AN OLD COUNTRY GIRL LIVES ON

My First 90 Years + 1 – Book 4

Bonnie Lacey Krenning

For information regarding permission, write to:
Starla Enterprises, Inc.
Attention: Permissions Department,
740 W. 2nd, Ste. 200, Wichita, KS 67203

First Edition

ISBN: 9798361629787

Edited by Starla Criser

Printed in the U.S.A.

DEDICATION

This story collection of my memories is a result of my life with many precious people.

My husband, William "Bill" John Krenning, supported and loved me for fifty-eight years. Not a day goes by that I don't think of him and our life together.

My children— John, Charlie, Kathie, and Suzie—helped give my life meaning. They have always made me proud to be their mother.

My grandchildren, great-grandchildren, and great-great-grandchildren are a special blessing that I will always treasure.

My parents, Anna and Herbert Lacey, made me into the woman I am today. They lived through difficult times but never gave up. They loved each of their many children. And they showed us not only to survive but to thrive, to appreciate, and to have fun and laugh.

ABOUT BONNIE LACEY KRENNING

After over nine decades of living, Bonnie is slowing down a little. She has led a challenging life and continues to treasure each day given to her.

Her husband, Bill, was her soulmate for fifty-eight years before he passed. Their family of four grown children, seven grandchildren, eleven great-grandchildren, three great-great-grandsons, and two great-great-granddaughters on the way this year are of key importance in her life.

Throughout her life, she has had many helpful pleasures, including sewing, gardening, and redecorating. Her dream of being a nurse since age six became a reality at age forty-eight.

Upon that graduation, Bill bought her a Cessna 150 as a special gift. Not long after that, at age fifty, she had the chance to fulfill another of her dreams, that of being a pilot.

In their many years toether, Bonnie and Bill had the opportunities to vacation throughout the united States. and she had the chance to go on mision trips to Ephesus and China.

TABLE OF CONTENTS

Chapter One
EPHESUS

An Exciting Opportunity.

In early spring 1999, I started seriously planning for our 50th Wedding Anniversary celebration and family reunion. I retired from my position as a school nurse and from full-time nursing when the school year was over.

At the same time, a friend from a local sister church told me about a mission trip some members of her church were taking in early August near Ephesus, Turkey. She asked if I would like to go with them as a nurse. A doctor was going, too, and there would be about fifteen men and women in our group. And Bill could go.

When I told him about the trip, he said, "No, I don't want to go, but you go for it!" He was in Europe during WW ll and didn't want to go overseas again.

Churches could not send missionaries to Turkey at that time. Workers, however, who were technicians in various fields and business and office personnel were much in demand. Teachers were also much requested, especially for elementary-age students in remote rural areas. Their employees paid the workers, but their income usually needed to be supplemented by our church denominations' Foreign Mission Board.

The workers could not openly witness their beliefs.

Still, as they became acquainted with the local people, they could discuss what they believed. Because of daily practicing their faith, the workers were sometimes asked and allowed to start Bible study groups and teach what they believed. The local people often came to accept Bible teachings.

Much of the work was in cities, offices, and other business settings. But teachers usually worked in remote rural areas. Some workers were married couples with children, and the families would go into the remote areas and start schools for all ages.

To maintain contact with each other, the workers met for a conference and planning convention for two weeks, every two years, at a resort close to Ephesus. Since most workers had children, our group was going there to do a Bible School each morning, four days a week, while the workers met in conference. Then the workers and our group would have time to enjoy the resort and take short bus trips and tours to Ephesus.

Our Foreign Mission Program paid for the meetings' expenses for us and the workers' conference. But each of us in our mission group paid our airplane travel expenses.

Preparation Begins.

Soon after our Family Reunion, our mission group started organizing the supplies we would need for the elementary school-age Bible School students. Most importantly, we would teach Bible stories with workbooks, and the kids would like the craft supplies for them. We would be singing choruses with one of our pianists playing for us.

At my church, the teenage girls' group I worked with

offered to make lace angel lapel pins as they had made for Valentine's Day for me to take on our trip. They attached the pins to a card with a Bible verse and gave them to friends and neighbors.

Together we made about two-hundred angel pins and attached them to cards. This time we could not put a Bible verse on the card, but I had been told the local people we would meet believed in angels. And most of them could read and speak English. We wrote on the angel cards, "Angels are watching over you." Our group handed the pins out to local women, teens, and kids.

Before we left on our trip, they advised us about the mission concerns to be aware of. They cautioned us about drinking local water, which may cause abdominal upset... yes, even diarrhea. We received bottled water. They also warned us not to eat raw fruits and vegetables for the same reason. It was usually a problem for mission groups going to another country.

When I worked in intensive care, patients were sometimes on tube feedings, usually developing diarrhea. With doctors' orders, the standard validated practice was to follow a tube feeding with a measure of fruit pectin in water through the feeding tube. The hospital purchased cases of fruit pectin from a local grocer to be kept available for the nurses to use.

As the nurse on our trip, I purchased an entire case of boxes of fruit pectin to take in a suitcase on our trip to prevent the problem. Fruit pectin is used in cooking to thicken jellies and jams, and that is why we purchased it from a grocery store. I told our group about using fruit pectin for diarrhea.

Traveling and Arrival.

Our trip was to last about three weeks, to allow travel time and getting settled in. We left out of the Wichita airport on Wednesday morning to the airport in New York City. We were so excited, and it was the first time most of us had been on a jet plane, much less headed for a foreign country.

After changing planes in New York City, we flew the several-hour trip. We landed at the airport in Istanbul, Turkey, Friday morning. By flying east, we lost several hours on the clock. A private bus took us the eighty miles to the resort near Ephesus, where we would be staying. There were rooms and apartments for hundreds of guests from all over the world.

Mission group - Bonnie on left in front row

Our group arrived at the resort about noon, hungry. But first, we had to get settled into our rooms with our luggage. On the trip, I became acquainted with a young schoolteacher and became friends. She and I shared a room and did our tours together.

The restaurant was in the middle of the resort, a proper centerpiece, a serve-yourself buffet. It was under a massive roof with the sides open. No air conditioning in August, but no one seemed to mind. We could eat whenever we wanted without extra cost to us.

The buffet included dozens of rows of foods, including meats, casseroles, soups, pasta, grains, and various cooked vegetables and fruits. There were rows of fresh salad choices, fruits, and a variety of desserts and drinks. We feasted then and for the rest of our time there.

Inside and outside, there were swimming pools and swimming at the seashore by the Aegean Sea. It was not unusual to see guests swimming totally nude. Yes, I said, "totally nude!" The kids usually didn't notice, and the adults... not so much.

The first evening we had a get-together with the workers and their children in the conference room where they would hold their meetings. They showed us the classroom where we would have Bible School for the children. It was a long but pleasant get-acquainted evening.

Adjusting to Eating Issues.

Before retiring, some of our group went to the buffet for an evening snack or more. Not me, and I was still feeling full, maybe too full. After such a busy day, my friend and I were ready to retire for the night.

I awakened early Saturday morning, excited about

taking our tour to Ephesus. But my stomach told me something was not right, and I hurried to the bathroom. I immediately added a heaping spoon of fruit pectin to a glass of water, stirred it, and sipped it. My friend and I decided not to go to Ephesus that day.

When we went to the restaurant, the resort had changed the food to a wonderful breakfast buffet. There were the usual breakfast meats, eggs and dishes, waffles, pancakes, cereals and juices, and other drinks. Our group and the workers and families loaded up their plates and sat at the tables under the roof. I ate carefully.

Soon I realized I needed to go to the bathroom. I again mixed another fruit pectin, stirred it, and drank it. Going to my room, I noticed some of our group using the outside restrooms and rushing to their rooms.

I again offered them the fruit pectin, but they went to the doctor for prescription medication instead. My diarrhea subsided, but the others had to stay close to a bathroom and could not go to lunch. I went to lunch but ate carefully.

Magical Fruit Pectin.

My friend had used the fruit pectin after first being seriously impacted and affected. It worked, and by Saturday evening, we were now moving about freely and eating at the buffet. The others in our group had not had lunch or supper. She and I had a restful night. But the others did not because they waited so long to use the fruit pectin.

The workers had church in the conference room on Sunday morning. My friend and I attended the service, but the others in our group were still recovering. The workers who lived there were not affected because they adapted to the food.

They cautioned our group to eat only cooked food and drink bottled water again. After using the fruit pectin treatment, most of them could eat a light lunch and spent a relaxing afternoon at the resort before eating an evening buffet. They all kept fruit pectin close by.

Our group spent a pleasant Sunday evening setting up for Bible School for the workers' children the following day and for the week. We were all able to do our job after a few days.

Starting Bible School.

Early Monday morning, our mission group was up and about, excited, and ready for the day. We visited with the workers and their children as we ate at the breakfast buffet. We were all prepared to start Bible School for the kids at nine o'clock.

Our group had prepared well. Each of us brought treats which we were told the kids liked and were not available where they lived. So, we took suitcases of individual packs of treats. I took one particular treat my grandkids liked: Goldfish crackers. I brought enough crackers for the kids to have them for treats several times. They were the kids' favorite treat.

The first morning of classes set the pattern for the

days to follow. We started with singing choruses, accompanied by the pianist. We taught Bible stories and encouraged the kids to memorize Bible verses to repeat at the closing ceremony for their parents. They did and enjoyed doing it. It was rewarding to see them having such a good time.

The kids enjoyed the craft supplies we brought, which included construction paper and crayons for drawing and coloring and scissors for cutting unusual patterns. We encouraged their unique creative designs. Then we closed the morning classes with more singing. At noon, the workers' conference and our Bible School dismissed for the day. We hurried to the buffet lunch together.

Children in Bible school class

Touring Historic Ephesus.

I was especially excited to start on our bus tour to Ephesus. I knew Paul and John of the New Testament had lived there during the first century. Some workers and their kids, and most of our group, took the trip in the afternoon, a few minutes' drive away. Our tour was in the historic part of Ephesus, as it was in the first century.

We got out of the bus and started the tour with our guide. The first site was the two-story front of a brick and stone library, still standing. The library had contained thousands of handwritten scripts. We were told by the guide that it was the first multi-language library in Asia Minor. Our tour group gathered in front of the standing library wall for pictures.

Group in front of first library

Then the guide showed us how far inland Ephesus is today. At the time Paul and John were there, it was a seaport. Over nearly twenty centuries, soil and sand had washed down to the seashore and Ephesus is now several miles inland.

We walked to the huge outdoor amphitheater where there were stage performances, and Paul and John often preached. The theater had stone seats placed on the hillsides that sat about 25,000 people. The theater is renowned for its perfect acoustics. There was no amplification. When speaking from the stage, we were told that all the audience could hear the speaker clearly and distinctly. We stood where Paul and

John stood when they preached. A memorable experience.

Ampitheater

Next on our tour was a large natural cave in a hillside where a theater had been installed. The domed cave ceiling was naturally about twenty-five feet high, and the room was large enough to seat several thousand in the seats they had put in place. They lit it with ornate oil lamps. The walls were a natural dark stone, so the theater was dimly lit. It had been much used for stage and musical performance groups throughout Asia Minor. The theater, being in a cave, was usually about the same temperature year-round, improving and increasing its use.

The guide showed us the large stone Physician's Symbol that marks the official beginning of the medical profession in the first century. He explained that the first University of Medicine in Asia Minor was in Ephesus.

Physician's Symbol

We were told there had been many hotels in the first century to accommodate guests coming from throughout Asia Minor. None of them were still standing. After a long, hot afternoon, we loaded onto our bus and headed back to the resort. Now hungry, we feasted at the buffet, then swam in the pools and at the beach by the Aegean Sea.

It had been an exciting day with our first Bible School and the first historic tour of Ephesus. Members of our group were all feeling well now and spent the evening eating and relaxing before retiring for the night. My friend and I, however, knew there were much more we wanted to see in Ephesus. We agreed to go back the next day.

Our Second Trip.

After Bible School for the kids and lunch at the buffet, my friend and I took the tour bus back to Ephesus to see what we had missed. There were English-speaking guides in place wherever we went.

We enjoyed browsing through the area where they still grow silkworms as they had in the first century, and before that. Silkworms are still a productive and lucrative business there. We watched women weaving the harvested silk yarn, dyed lovely colors, into beautiful oriental and other decorative rugs. Only the wealthy could afford the rugs.

As we continued walking, we came upon an area where there was a small outdoor stage and kitchenette area, with wooden table and stools close by. The guide there explained that in the first century in Ephesus, they could not see women and children out in public. Business and professional men gathered there for breakfast. Cooks—men—prepared breakfast for them, while musicians and singers entertained the men.

We noticed there were benches made of stone slabs off to the side. The seats had stone fronts. There were several holes, a few inches across, in the seats. Once more, the guide explained that after the men ate a big breakfast and drank their coffee, they moved around as they chose to the benches, using the holes for their "morning constitution." After all, there were no women and children around.

Bonnie and friend on bench

Done with our tour, we took the bus back to the resort. After a delicious and filling buffet, we enjoyed another relaxing evening, reminiscing about the day's tour.

Seven Churches Tour.

Our group was so pleased and excited to be at the resort near historical Ephesus for our mission trip to do Bible School for the kids. There were so many cruises, trips, and places where we could go in our free time.

I heard about a tour of the Seven Churches of the Book of Revelation, written by John in the New Testament. Because it was only on a day when we were having Bible School we couldn't go. It disappointed me to not take the tour to the churches I had studied and learned about in the Bible.

Not going as I wanted turned out to be a good thing. Later I learned that my cousin and her husband had taken the tour to the Seven Churches. She told me that the church buildings were no longer there. Only memorial signs, stones and rubble were in place as their tour group was told of the history of the churches.

Cruise to Patmos.

I learned about another trip, a one-day cruise on the Aegean Sea to the Isle of Patmos. And the cruise was on Friday when we were out of Bible School for the kids. When I mentioned it to our group, at first no one was interested in going. But as I continued talking…. and talking…. about the cruise, they all decided to go. Most of the workers and their kids took the cruise with us. It was a big ship and there were about two hundred passengers.

After an early breakfast our group, the workers and their kids were excited to board the ship anchored close to the resort. There were also many other passengers who were guests at the resort from throughout the world.

Cruise ship to Isle of Patmos

They furnished the main deck of the ship with tables and chairs for the passenger, with refreshments available.

I walked over to the side rails and saw the beautiful

dark blue green water. Though the water was dark, it was clear. With the sun shining brightly, I could plainly see the rock formations at the bottom of the sea. The rocks looked like they were a few feet away. I spoke to the guide about the clear water and rocks. He told me that the rocks were hundreds of feet down. The clear water only made it look like they were close.

After admiring the scene for a while, I took the stairs to the open-air upper deck, where our group gathered and enjoyed the view from there. There were uninhabited rock islands in all directions. I tried to imagine how the ship could navigate its way to Patmos but didn't doubt it could.

It was interesting visiting with the passengers from other countries. Most of them spoke English. We talked about where we were from and why we were there. They were usually dignitaries, political leaders, and business and professional people.

The August sun was getting hot, so I wandered back down the stairs to the main deck. On the stairs, I noticed the ship's pilot, sitting with his hands on the ship's steering wheel. I strolled over to where he was and spoke to him. He smiled and answered in broken English.

I asked him about the wall of instruments in front of him. He began explaining as I stood at a distance. Then he motioned for me to come closer. He got up and insisted that I sit in his chair and "steer the ship."

Reluctantly, but intrigued, I sat down and took hold of the steering wheel. I didn't dare turn it, certain he had his instruments set. After a few minutes, I relinquished the steering wheel, stood up, and stepped away. He took his seat as we shared smiles, and I moved on.

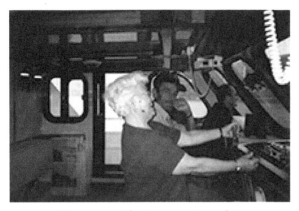

Bonnie piloting cruise ship

Looking out across the waters, I saw the Isle of Patmos ahead of us. There were cathedrals, castles, and other large, ancient buildings in view. About mid-morning, we docked the ship and all the passengers walked out onto the island together.

We went with a guide to show us the historic sites. There were museums of hand-written scripts written in many languages. Most of them did not use our alphabet. With the guide's informative and pleasant talks, it was an interesting tour.

They had held John of the New Testament, who wrote the Book of Revelation, there as a political prisoner for several years. They did not hold him in a cell because miles of deep water surrounded the island and there was no way to escape. The surrounding islands were uninhabited, so escaping would mean certain death.

They showed us a six-foot cave where John lived. While there in the cave, he wrote the Book of Revelation of the New Testament.

One thing I was looking forward to while on the Greek Island was the chance to eat in a Greek restaurant. When lunchtime came, our group walked around together, surveying the choices. They overruled me. The others decided to go to McDonalds. I went with them.

After lunch, we continued exploring the historic museums and beautiful cathedrals. We boarded the ship for our ride back to the resort in the late afternoon. We were pleasantly exhausted, but it had been a good idea for us to take the trip to Patmos.

Visiting with the Local People.

Saturday, the next day after our trip to Patmos, was the first day our group didn't have Bible School, church services or tours. We relaxed and visited with others, especially the local people. Most of them spoke English and seemed eager to talk with us. They were the women who cleaned our rooms, the men who cleaned the grounds, and the many workers who tended the buffets.

I've spoken so much about the buffets. They were in the center of the resort, with our hotel rooms close by. The buffet offerings were not fast food; many delicious foods we had never eaten before. We historically knew Turkey for its fine cuisine. We were told that Paris, in the eighteen-hundreds, sent their culinary artists and cooks to Istanbul eighty miles north of Ephesus to learn their method of cuisine.

When we first arrived at the resort, I distributed to our group the lace angel lapel pins I brought. The teenage girls back home had attached each pin to a card that read: "Angels are watching over you" and put them in individual plastic bags. We were told that most of the local people believed in angels. As we gave the local woman an angel pin, they seemed pleased and excited to get one. They asked us questions about our God and guardian angels. They were eager to listen and talk to us.

George Washington's Blue Eyes.

I liked to walk about the resort grounds and visit, especially with local people. I noticed they tinted their black hair henna red: women, men, and children. We were told they grew the henna plant that was used worldwide for tinting hair in Turkey. The tint was attractive, yes, even on men.

Out walking one afternoon, I noticed a young man at an outdoor ice cream cone stand under the shade of a tree. He looked like he was about college age. He had naturally tan skin and henna tinted hair. As I came closer, he started smiling.

Before I could order an ice cream cone, he asked me where I was from, speaking excellent English. When I told him from the United States, he asked where in the United States. I told him Kansas, and he described where Kansas was in the United States. He said he had been to college in New York City.

As we were talking, I noticed he had bright blue eyes. The local people all had dark brown eyes. At the first break in our conversation, I asked, "Where did you get your blue eyes?"

With a whimsical grin, he said, "George Washington." Customers were lining up to get their ice cream cones.

23

Smiling, the young man turned and began serving them.

I walked away without my ice cream cone. It was obvious that some of his ancestors had spent time in the United States or other foreign countries. *But, George Washington?*

Our Final Days There.

Our group started our second week with both morning and evening Sunday church services, and a prayer meeting Wednesday night led by the workers. They thanked us for doing Bible School for their kids so they could meet in conference. The workers and our group never missed a chance to get together. It was a great time of fellowship.

The following week, during morning Bible School, the kids memorized and practiced for the closing ceremony on Thursday evening. I'll admit I had thought about our trip home and being with my family and friends. I missed Bill and we still had several days before leaving. But it was a fun week. No more tours. Just relaxing, visiting, swimming, and eating. The week went by fast.

We spent Thursday packing our personal suitcases and the Bible School luggage. The closing ceremony that night was a lot of fun. The kids enjoyed reciting their memory verses and singing the choruses they learned. They were eager to show and gather the crafts they had made. We visited together, knowing it would be the last time we would see the workers and their kids. A sad moment, but none of us would forget our time here.

McDonald's is Everywhere.

Very early Friday morning, we ate a final wonderful buffet breakfast. Then we loaded onto a bus just for our group. It would take us the eighty miles to the Istanbul Airport for our flight home.

The scenery was beautiful with farm crops of many kinds in the fields. I noticed there were no farmhouses, just rare mansions back from the highway. We were told by the guide that the land was owned by wealthy farmers. The farmhands lived in high-rise apartments in the city. They furnished transportation for the workers to get to the fields each day, from daylight to dusk.

It was annoying, though, to have huge advertising signs all along the highway. Most of the signs were for fast foods. The largest and most colorful were the McDonald's signs. On the eighty-mile drive, there were over twenty such signs.

An Angel Pins Siting.

When we arrived at the airport, our guide walked us through the large airport to where we would board our plane to go home.

Oh! Can this be? While we were walking through the airport, we noticed some men, yes men, walking around in dress suits. They were wearing a lace angel pin on the lapel of their suit jacket next to their necktie. We saw over a dozen men wearing pins. *Who knows where in the world our pins may have gone?*

Back in the Good Old USA.

Our group loaded on the plane to take us to the New York City airport. Because we were flying west, we gained back the time we had "lost" on our trip when we flew east. At the NYC airport, we were excited to have a close connection for our flight to Wichita.

Upon landing at the airport in Wichita, a church bus was there to take us back to the church. We loaded all our luggage and headed to where our families were waiting to welcome us back to the "Good Old USA!"

I was experiencing jet lag and pure exhaustion. And I was so hungry for Bill's cooking. Guess what? He had a wonderful meal prepared for me with the foods he knew I liked. The resort buffet could not compare to it. We spent a quiet evening just relaxing together, knowing they would expect and welcome us at church in the morning.

Our pastor contacted each of our mission group on Monday morning, asking us to get together on Wednesday afternoon to discuss our trip. That afternoon we spent a couple of hours talking about our mission work and getting to know the workers. Then we shared our memories about our tours of Ephesus, the Isle of Patmos, and our fun at the resort.

Finally, our pastor asked, "What was the most important thing you learned on the trip?"

The young church secretary that went with us raised her hand and clearly stated, "Take fruit pectin when you have diarrhea!"

We all laughed and clapped. I believe the fruit pectin saved our workers from being so sick they would not have been able to do Bible School for the kids.

I will always remember my first mission trip overseas, my first flight overseas.

Chapter Two
ON THE ROAD AGAIN

Our Love of Traveling.

I enjoyed the mission trip, but it took a few days to adjust to the jet lag afterward. When our kids and grandkids spent time with us before school started that fall, it helped me settle back into being home. We spent a lot of time visiting and talking about my trip experiences. There was the regular swimming and feasting, and Bill kept the food and treats coming.

Bill and I wanted to have our church members out for a potluck supper and swimming party on a Sunday evening before it got cold. They were excited to come. And it allowed our church to use the event for outreach to invite guests. Our usual church attendance was about fifty people, and the attendance at our party was over one hundred people. We welcomed all.

Everyone brought food, but our pastor became increasingly concerned that there wasn't enough. As he often did, Bill came to the rescue. He had large cans of pork and beans, packages of beanie weenies, and other foods, which he thawed out, so no one went hungry.

As things quieted down, Bill and I started discussing where we would like to take a trip, or trips, that fall. For the five years I was a school nurse, we couldn't go on trips in the fall or spring when the weather was good and not too hot or too cold.

He would go anywhere if he could drive there. He wanted and was eager to be "on the road again." We both enjoyed learning about our country's history and were interested in visiting historical sites. Even though we liked traveling, we never wanted to be away from home and our family for over two weeks, so we came and went a lot.

The Medicine Lodge Reenactment.

I knew about the Medicine Lodge Peace Treaty in 1867 in what would become western Kansas. The Treaty was between the United States Government and several Native American tribes. A reenactment of the Treaty took place every September at the site about eighty miles from Wichita. We decided that would be a good time to go there.

The reenactment site was at the exact place where the treaty took place. It was a natural amphitheater in a vast field, several miles long and wide. There was a natural north hillside with seats in place for the observers on the hillside. Bill and I took seats where we could see for miles.

In the early afternoon, we watched covered wagons pulled by horses, and uniformed riders mounted on horses emerge into the amphitheater from the east. Then Native Americans in full, colorful Indian attire rode in on horseback from the west. Altogether, there were hundreds of men "on stage."

As they approached each other, riders from both sides

rode out in front and conversed. Interpreters spoke both English and tribal languages, and we could plainly hear them through amplified speakers. The whole reenactment lasted about two hours. It was an outstanding, authentic, and fascinating display of history. We felt as though we had attended the original signing of the treaty.

While there, we became aware of another full day of activities the following day. We quickly decided to go back the next day.

A Parade and A Hanging.

We drove the eighty miles back, arriving in time to watch the parade in Medicine lodge. It was not the usual parade, and there were marching bands and different tribes of Indians in their native dress. Mingled throughout the parade were "sheriffs," "cowboys," and "outlaw gunfighters," chasing and shooting at each other.

After the parade, we went to an outdoor stage show featuring musicians, singers, and dancing girls in colorful costumes. The audience sat in chairs on the lawn, and Bill and I took seats at one end of the front row. While the dancers performed, we heard gunfire from across the audience on the other side.

We turned to see a "sheriff" chasing an "outlaw." The outlaw turned, and they shot each other. "Blood" ran from their wounds as they fell to the ground. Other sheriffs gathered around them and dragged their bodies away.

We had noticed a hanging noose in that area. There was another commotion, and two uniformed men dragged a screaming and yelling man onto a platform. They placed the noose around his neck.

Holding tightly to the rope, they yanked it, lifting the man off the platform. They left him hanging, writhing, and twisting. Then his body went limp.

They lowered the body to the ground and dragged him out of sight. The "pretend hanging" had been very realistic.

Bill's Playacting.

Meanwhile, the stage show went on as though nothing bad had happened. We turned to watch the dancers for a while. Suddenly, they started moving down the steps at the side of the stage, and Bill and I were sitting close by.

One dancer came over to Bill and reached out her hand to him. Smiling, she said, "Come and dance with me!"

Bill stayed sitting. He grimaced and grabbed his thigh. "I can't! They shot me in the leg!" he moaned.

The dancer threw up her arms and stepped back, looking shocked. "Really?" she exclaimed.

Bill smiled, and she realized he had tricked her. Understanding he didn't want to dance with her, she moved on into the audience to dance with someone else.

With the stage show over, we realized we were hungry and thirsty. The aromas from the food stands were enticing. There were hamburgers and hot dogs, but we wanted to try the special foods and drinks of the different tribes. While we feasted, we watched as several tribes danced in their Pow Wows. They played their drums, danced, and sang in their tribal languages. Even though we couldn't understand them, we enjoyed the sounds and the beauty of the performances.

By late afternoon, we were ready to head home. We planned to return for both days next year. And we did.

Catching Up at Home.

Back home, Bill mowed the two-acre church lawn and our two-acre lawn with his riding lawnmower. It took most of the day. At lunch, I noticed he didn't seem to enjoy the task/chore as usual. He said he needed to cut firewood for our temperature-controlled fireplace he inserted to heat our house in the wintertime. And he had other tasks.

As he started looking for wood to cut, he decided we had enough wood on hand for the fireplaces. He seemed relieved by the decision. He still had to keep the swimming pool cleaned for all our guests. To Bill's delight, they often complimented him about how clean our pool was.

I spent my time relaxing and enjoying swimming, working on my flowers, and cooking as I wished. Besides Bill's other tasks, he conditioned our cars, our kids', and grandkids' cars, and sometimes friends' and neighbors' cars. Everyone knew him for his ability to troubleshoot cars, especially older ones. He often volunteered, sometimes too much.

After spending a couple of weeks with family and friends, Bill was anxious to get on the road again. He asked me where I would like to go, and I said, "Santa Fe, New Mexico." So, he mowed the lawns for the last time that fall, and we packed our suitcases and headed out.

Our Time in Santa Fe.

We arrived in Santa Fe in the early afternoon and checked into the vintage hotel room I had reserved. There were many landmark sights, and we were excited to see them.

One intriguing building was an old-fashioned church. A guide walked us through the ornate church, stopping by a decorative metal freestanding spiral stairway. He said it is an unsolved mystery how the stairway can remain standing and not fall.

We ended our day with a lovely evening at a traditional restaurant. They served the usual menu, but they also specialized in various local and native foods. We spent a long night there, savoring the foods before retiring to rise early for the tours we came for.

I had already learned that before New Mexico was New Mexico, it was in the Midwest area where many Native American tribes had lived for centuries. Before the arrival of the white man and the Indians being forced onto reservations, their communities were called Pueblo settlements.

In the last few decades, the Indian tribes could return to their original pueblos, live there, and replant original crops. They reinstated their original attire, crafts, Pow Wows, and religious ceremonies. Not having electricity, the natives cooked over open fires and had designed ovens for baking their bread.

There were bus tours daily out of Santa Fe going east, south, west, and north to the reestablished pueblos. I signed us up for each day of the four tours. Bill rarely liked to take bus tours but agreed to go with me, and each trip took several hours.

When we arrived at a pueblo, our guide explained the unique culture of the tribe there. The Indians lived in tents or in hillside caves when available. They favored caves because they were cool in summer and warmer in the winter.

Most of the natives spoke some English, and we visited with them. We also enjoyed their singing, dancing, and playing their drums. Best of all was the delicious native foods they served us, prepared on their open fires and ovens. Each day was a joyous and unique learning experience. And Bill enjoyed the tours, too.

The fourth day was the most unique of all. It was the north pueblo just outside of Santa Fe. As we arrived at the pueblo, we noticed a steep hillside on the north with many large caves. In front of the caves, a large area had many tents occupied by the natives who lived and worked there.

Our guide then told us that there were a few Indians employed outside the pueblo but lived in a cave or tent. Just before we left, an Indian in a suit and tie walked in from where he had parked his car about a mile away. He walked into a cave and soon came out in native attire.

The north site was the only pueblo where they sold arts and crafts to the visitors. They had booths set up where the artists made and sold native jewelry of silver, turquoise, and other rare stones. So, I bought a unique silver and turquoise necklace. After twenty years, I still wear it often, and it is always much admired.

One of the most unique sites at the pueblo was a small stone Catholic church. Our guide said they built it in the sixteen-hundreds, and it has stood silent for many years.

Our trip was a wonderful experience, far beyond my

expectations. After finishing our fourth tour, though, we were both ready to return home. And Bill was eager to get on the road again.

Chapter Three
HOME FOR A WHILE

A Trip to the Country.

It was always good to be back home again. If things weren't happening, we started making them happen.

Black walnuts are essential to this squirrelly story.

John and his wife, Cindy, and little Mark had moved to the country, and John built a nice, energy-efficient house on a small acreage next to Cindy's parents. Her parents had both retired and enjoyed country living, and little Mark was enjoying his grandparents.

One lovely autumn afternoon, we, Mark's other grandparents, visited John and his family. We took a walk down by the creek on Cindy's parent's place. It was a pleasant walk among lots of trees with the many colors of fall: fading green, yellow, orange, and red. And the air smelled fresh mixed with decaying fallen leaves.

I noticed the black walnut trees, and lots of walnuts had fallen to the ground. I told Cindy's parents that black walnuts were my favorites from my childhood. They said we could take all we wanted if we picked them up.

Bill and I went back the following Sunday afternoon, and I picked up two five-gallon buckets of black walnuts. Now that we had black walnuts, I would add the nutmeats to the fudge I had made since I was twelve years old. The recipe was on the back of a Hershey's Cocoa can. When I added the black walnut meats to the fudge, it was more delicious than ever. I found myself making the fudge often for our family and guests. I also added them to cookies. Of course, there would be enough extra nutmeats for snacks.

Bill loaded the full buckets in the back of his pickup, and we headed for home. He set the buckets out on the garage floor. We were aware of the many squirrels playing in the tree close by and how they often scampered about the yard. They would sometimes sit on the wooden plank pool fence and watch Bill as he worked.

Mischief Makers.

The next day, as Bill was working in the garage, he realized the squirrels were jumping up on the rims of the buckets and picking up a walnut. They scampered away to their nest in the trees to store their treats for winter. So, Bill picked the buckets up and set them in his boat nearby.

That didn't stop the squirrels. They scampered up into the boat, picked up a walnut, and carried it away to their nest.

Bill put lids on the buckets. The squirrels came into the garage close by him and looked at him, seeming anxious and annoyed that he had spoiled their fun.

The squirrels' behavior fascinated him. Hoping to keep them around and close by, he went to a store that sold bulk nuts and other foods. He bought several pounds of peanuts in the shell. Then he fashioned shallow containers, which he filled with peanuts and hung on the pool fence.

The squirrels found the peanuts and quickly carried them off to their nests. Within a few days, they had carried all the peanuts away.

Bill went back to the nut store, and he noticed they had peanuts in the cracked shell, so he bought several pounds.

When the squirrels found the peanuts, they would grab one and jump up on the fence. The squirrel would break open the shell and crunch on the peanut while sitting there. They didn't carry the nuts to their nests in the trees.

Mutual Curiosity.

It delighted us when the squirrels became more and more friendly. One day, I was working at the kitchen sink, looking out the large window at the lovely view of the lake. Suddenly, a squirrel jumped up on the outside windowsill. He/she raised up on their hind legs and placed their front paws on the window glass. It seemed it smiled at me before scampering away.

Our dinette area, by the kitchen, opened through an outside door onto the swimming pool area. The squirrels would come up to the sliding door, raise up on their hind legs and place their front paws on the glass, looking into the dinette area.

We had a large, ornate, wrought-iron dinette set with six chairs. One day, I had an idea. I opened the sliding glass door and pulled a chair across the room. I sat down, holding out a cracked peanut in my fingers.

Soon a squirrel came to the open door, hurried across the room, and took the peanut from my fingers. He scampered out and jumped up on the fence, and he sat there as he shelled the cracked peanut and crunched on it.

Bill's brother Bud and his wife, Norma, came for a visit. She was a country girl, and she had never lived in the city and was used to the ways of squirrels. When I told her about the squirrels coming into the room, she seemed amazed and unbelieving and wanted to try it out.

It surprised her when a squirrel came into the room and took a peanut from her fingers. She tried the procedure several times before they left.

It was a "game" our kids, grandkids, and friends loved to play, usually continuously when they were visiting. The squirrels always seemed ready to "participate."

Bill's Change in Attitude.

Bill was just six years old when he started shooting squirrels for family food in the trees close to their home in the country, using his mom's four-ten shotgun. He began hunting squirrels with his dad in his early teens with a rifle. Then he hunted squirrels with his brother and friends when he was growing up. He was known to get a squirrel with every bullet. Of course, for food.

One day, Bill and I were relaxing in our lawn chairs out by the pool. He was quiet, seeming remorseful as he watched the squirrels scamper and play with each other. In a soft voice, he quietly said, "I just don't know how I ever shot those little guys."

While we lived in the country for many years, Bill continued feeding his squirrels each year until late fall, when they hibernated in their nests in the trees until spring. One regret we had when we moved back to town was leaving the squirrels. "They would not have Bill's peanuts."

Scalding a Hawg!

Our trips had been enjoyable, but now it was time to settle down at home for the rest of the year.

Most days that fall, I swam in our pool's cool/chilly waters. Usually, I hurried into our bathroom and turned on the whirlpool bathtub. After stripping off my bathing suit, I soaked in the hot sauna bath as steam floated out into the room.

One day, as Bill came into the bathroom, he saw the thick steam. He hollered, "Good grief! That water is hot enough to scald a hawg!"

I knew he was referring to the scalding water they used when he was a child to butcher a hog. It wasn't quite that hot, and I continued to do the hot saunas after my cold swim until he closed the pool.

Simple Exercise.

Bill mowed the church lawn and our lawn for the last time that fall. After that, he kept busy helping with or doing most of the cleaning. I helped with that, too, unless I was relaxing. I also kept busy knitting, hand-quilting, and working on my flowers.

Bill started walking two miles around the lake when we moved to the country, several mornings a week before breakfast. After I retired, I started walking with him most of the time. It was a pleasant time for both of us. His doctor said that he didn't need to continue rehab after his bypass surgery because of his walking. Bill walked in bad weather and snow, but never in the rain.

My Skating Days Ended.

When I was about six years old, I watched kids skating at the new roller-skating rink in town. I didn't skate that day, but I wanted to learn how to skate someday. The chance didn't come until I was fourteen years and we moved to Rich Hill, Missouri, and l learned to skate.

When I met Bill at sixteen, we spent most of our dates roller-skating. He had learned to skate while he was in basic training in the army. Bill skated forward. While holding his hand, I slid backward, doing twists and turns. Then beside him in each other's arms, we swayed to one side, then the other. Bill smiled, seeming to enjoy himself. I was.

I learned after we were married that he didn't really like to roller-skate. So, Bill and I never skated together again. When our kids were big enough, I took them skating with me until they were old enough to decline. Occasionally, I went alone.

After a few years in the country, I solved my skating problem. I bought a pair of white rollerblade skates and took them home, excited to skate again. Our community's south side paved roads had gradual inclines and declines between the straight roads. The roads were not paved on the far side of the lake, so that I couldn't skate around the lake.

When Bill was busy doing his chosen tasks or relaxing, I would put on my rollerblades and skate for an hour. As I skated through our neighborhood, I enjoyed greeting the friendly and sometimes surprised neighbors as I skated along without stopping.

During the several years of rollerblading, I had taken a few tumbles, nothing serious, and I didn't tell Bill. One day while skating down an incline, I lost my balance. I went down easily, but maybe it jolted my reasoning.

After skating home, I took off the rollerblades. I was sixty-eight years old, and it was time to stop outdoor roller skating. I gave the skates to a grown-up great-granddaughter.

Bill's Secret Stew.

Bill enjoyed cooking and baking, making sure the freezer was fully stocked. He liked welcoming our many guests, both expected and unexpected. He planned to have a meal ready to set on the table quickly, at any time.

He became known for his delicious, yes scrumptious, beef stew. Bill had developed his own recipe, but never wrote it down.

Bill's Stew
He varied it from time-to-time, as he wished.
First, he cut a lean beef roast up into bite-sized pieces, trimmed off all the fat, dusted the pieces with flour and his secret seasonings. Then he sauteed the pieces until they were well-browned in greased cast iron skillets.

Next, he dumped the pieces and canned tomatoes in an eight-quart pot to about half full. He added water and simmered it for about two hours to tenderize the meat.
While the meat simmered, he cut up a full head of cabbage and added it to the pot.
He continued cutting up and adding potatoes, carrots, peas, sweet peppers, celery, onions, and other vegetables until the pot was full to running over.
After simmering the stew for a couple of hours, he let it cool down and poured it into containers for the freezer.

One day, as it cooked and Bill stirred, I noticed the pot was full to nearly running over. When I asked him if he would like a bigger pot, he assured me with a smile that he would. So, I bought him a ten-quart pot that matched the other pots in our set.

Within a short time, he had the new pot full to almost running over. So, I bought him a twelve-quart pot. Bill smiled when he saw the latest pot. As he used it, he still filled it but was careful not to run it over. I quit buying him bigger pots.

The task took Bill most of the day, but he loved making the stew and was pleased that most everyone liked it.

Bill continued to make his stew until shortly before his passing. I tried to make his beef stew a few times but never came close to Bill's "secret" delicious stew. I know for sure, and others agreed that my stew was not as good as Bill's.

Our Thanksgiving Tradition.

It was time to plan and prepare for our family's

expected Thanksgiving dinner. Since I retired, it was the first time Bill and I could shop together for what we needed.

For many years, our family met on the Saturday before Thanksgiving. When our kids and grandkids arrived, the house smelled of the dinner already waiting. We prepared a large turkey with brown rice dressing and gravy, vegetables, and salads, to mention a few items. Bill baked his brownies and pumpkin pies to serve with whipped cream. And I made yeast rolls and cinnamon rolls.

Bill's Brownies
One day someone asked Bill for his brownie recipe. He smiled and said, "Me and Betty Crocker make 'em."
He added chocolate chips and nutmeats to the Betty Crocker brownie mix, spread the mix out into a baking pan.
Then he sprinkled the top with nutmeats.
These were the most delicious brownies I ever tasted.

As was our family tradition, we joined hands in prayer and sat down at our table. Some grandkids sat at side tables. We talked and laughed together throughout the long meal and the desserts. It took a while for us to "recover" from stuffing ourselves.

The small grandkids played with their toys. The rest of us talked and laughed together until someone started singing Christmas carols. Soon we all joined in, some of us singing in parts while others sang off-key. We no longer had our Steinway grand piano but didn't miss it as we continued to sing with gusto acapella.

At the same time, some of us cleared the table and stacked dishes in the dishwasher, and we washed pots and pans in the sink. When evening came, and our families were getting ready to head home, we sent loads of our extra food with them.

Bill and I were ready to rest, watching holiday movies on TV. After a good night's rest, we went to church. They had a potluck dinner, and Bill had prepared a favorite casserole to take. The next few days before the actual Thanksgiving Day, he and I relaxed together.

The Mall and Us.

Bill gladly helped me put up our "permanent" Christmas tree that didn't shed needles the day after Thanksgiving. We spent a couple of days decorating the tree and putting up decorations throughout the house.

Our "forever" Christmas tree

This year, I had not done our Christmas shopping by catalog, planning to shop at the new mall. Bill didn't like shopping at the mall, and I told him I would do my shopping there, thinking he might want some free time from me.

To my surprise, Bill quickly said, "I'll go with you." And he seemed glad to do so.

One morning, we headed out to the mall, and I had a list of each family member and what they might like for Christmas. Bill walked around with me as I shopped, helping to carry the many bags of gifts. Then we got hungry for lunch.

The middle of the mall had a food court with tables and chairs. There were many excellent choices of foods: Asian, Mexican, and others. Bill told me his selection of foods and sat down at a table with our bags. I liked walking by the serving area, making the choices for us. We enjoyed sitting there to rest, eating, and talking before heading home.

I wanted to go back to the mall the next day. Bill was ready and willing but suggested that he sit at a table in the food court, and I could shop as I wished and bring the gifts back for him to watch as I continued shopping.

This worked out well. Bill enjoyed watching the shoppers come and go as I shopped. We again ate lunch there before heading home. We enjoyed a couple more shopping trips to the mall to complete our Christmas gift list. It took several hours for Bill and me to wrap the twenty or so gifts and place them under our Christmas tree.

We spent many hours relaxing and watching Christmas programs on TV during the holiday season between our many shopping trips for gifts.

Another Year Over.

Then it was time to shop for our family's Christmas

dinner. Bill always kept a shopping list. When I mentioned we needed something, he'd say, "Write it on the list!"

We prepared a large, boneless ham with candied sweet potatoes, mashed potatoes, turkey gravy, colorful vegetable dishes, and salads. Bill always made his deluxe brownies and beautiful pecan pies. I made my expected sweet rolls, cinnamon rolls, and Bill's favorite of all my desserts: apple pies.

Bill's Pecan Pies

Bill considered all recipes to be "suggestions." I no longer have his pecan pie recipe and am not sure what exactly he added to make it so delicious. Each pie was a work of art.
He placed pecan halves in circles on top of the pie, so it was covered, before baking it.
The pies were good keepers, so Bill usually had one or more pies ready for us.

I didn't think it was possible, but our Christmas that year felt like the best ever. Everyone seemed pleased with their gifts. Our kids and grandkids had such busy lives, and it was special to have the time to be together.

We handled the Christmas dinner much the same way as at Thanksgiving. After holding hands in prayer in thanks for each other and what we were blessed with, we served our dinner buffet style. We loaded our plates and sat wherever we wished. Some of the little ones sat on the comfortable, padded carpet.

After eating, relaxing, and visiting for a while, someone started singing a Christmas carol. We all joined in singing a cappella, even those who could not carry a tune. As we sang, some of us began gathering the food and packing bags for our families to take home, another of our traditions.

Exhausted but content, Bill and I spent our evening relaxing in our recliners, watching TV before retiring. We went to our Sunday Christmas church service the following day and attended the potluck dinner afterward. Again, Bill took a favorite casserole.

New Year's Eve was still several days away, but I persuaded Bill to leave our Christmas tree up until then. We spent the day boxing decorations from the tree and throughout the house. It was always a little sad to see Bill box our tree and pack it away until the next year.

1999 was over. It had been an eventful, more than a busy year. Now, Bill and I could quietly relax at home and start making plans for 2000.

Chapter Four
BACK ON THE ROAD

A Quiet Time.

Bill and I enjoyed some quiet time together for a couple of weeks after New Year's Day. It had been months since we did that. We enjoyed watching TV as I knitted and hand quilted. I had to be doing something. Bill, not so much, just relaxing and sometimes dosing.

While taking things slowly at home, we were involved in our church activities. I taught Bible classes and attended women's groups. Bill kept active, serving on finance and maintenance committees, and mowing the church lawn. He also put some of his recipes in the cookbook the women published.

Though we hadn't mentioned it, I know we were both thinking about our road trips that spring. For years, I had heard about the Mardi Gras festival every year in New Orleans, Louisiana, before Easter Lent. There was rowdy Cajun music and dancing in the streets and sideshows. And I had heard that the Cajun food there was some of the most delicious in the country.

Our Mardi Gras Experience.

When I mentioned the idea of a road trip there to Bill, he was ready and eager to drive us to New Orleans and experience the festivities. I rented a hotel room ahead of time. The rooms were scarce and pricy because people came to the festival from other countries.

We loaded our suitcases and headed out. It was a day-long drive from Wichita, and we only stopped for lunch. When we left home, there were no signs of spring yet. But as we moved south, the dogwood, redbud, and flowering fruit trees were in full bloom. The beautiful scenery on the trip was worth the drive.

Approaching New Orleans in the evening, the Cajun music and singing was in the air. We checked into our hotel room and were hungry for a good Cajun dinner in a nice restaurant. While eating, we watched through a large window the people celebrating in the streets. They were singing, dancing and, oh yes, drinking, maybe excessively. After our long day, Bill and I retired to our hotel room for a good night's rest, eager to explore the following day.

The next morning, we went to the festivities to eat a Cajun breakfast from the many food stands. Two blocks of the main street of New Orleans were blocked off from traffic for the festival. The street was already packed with people, and some were entertainers, but most were visitors like us.

People played instruments of all kinds, singing and dancing in the street. It seemed like everyone was wearing colorful costumes except us. There were lots of alcoholic beverage stands. We noticed that many people had a drink in their hand, and some had already over imbibed.

Bill and I spent the day walking around the two-block area, listening to stage shows of lively Cajun music. We feasted on the deliciously spicy food throughout the day. That evening we attended an indoor stage show. Individuals and groups were in elaborate, colorful costumes, singing and dancing on stage.

That night in our hotel room, we tiredly agreed the trip to Mardi Gras had been worth the long drive. We had filled the day with exciting, unique experiences that we would remember. We also agreed that one trip to the festival was enough. It was time to head home to our peaceful life.

A Childhood Dream.

As a small child, I liked learning the history of our country. I memorized our presidents' names in order of their terms in office. They lived in fancy houses, and I wanted to go see them. I didn't know how far away they were or how I would ever get there. Then Bill came along, and he made it all happen for me.

One day as we were eating lunch, Bill asked me if there was someplace I wanted to go before he opened the swimming pool in a couple of weeks. Yes! I had been planning in my mind our next trip. So, I told him about it.

Abraham Lincoln was my most admired president. I wanted to visit his birthplace in Kentucky, then go on to Springfield, Illinois, where he later lived. He then became an attorney and, later, our president.

It just so happened that President Andrew Jackson's

Hermitage plantation home was along the way in Tennessee. The Hermitage was open to tourists on certain days. When I told Bill, he readily agreed to go there as well. The following Monday, we headed out on our trip.

A Private Tour of The Hermitage.

As we traveled, the spring scenery was breathtaking. The houses in the many small towns along the way had flower beds with masses of colorful blooming flowers. Driving further south, we observed all kinds of wildflowers blooming in the fields and forests. The trees were leafing out, and some of the flowering trees were still blooming, which we didn't see on our Kansas plains.

We didn't plan to see the Hermitage that day and stayed in a nearby motel that night. The following day, we drove to the mansion. Bill pulled up in front and said, "Look, there are no other cars around." He started to drive away.

I hollered, "Stop! Let me go check if there is someone in there."

He stopped, and I walked up to the massive, ornate front door and knocked. An elderly man came to the door. He said, "We're not open on weekdays, only on weekends."

Disappointed, I told the man we had come all the way from Wichita, Kansas, to see the Hermitage. He graciously agreed to let us go in and tour the mansion.

Bill and I walked inside, and the man and a couple of women in casual attire welcomed us. They showed us the many elegant bedrooms, formal front parlor, and huge dining room. They told us that President Jackson and his family had entertained many guests at the Hermitage.

Having not seen the kitchen and being curious about it, I asked where it was. The guides showed us a separate, one-room building close to the dining-room door. They explained that slave cooks prepared the food there and carried it inside so the kitchen would not heat the mansion in the long, hot summers in the south.

The man told Bill about the history of the two-story mansion. It was built by educated and accomplished slave carpenters. When Bill showed interest, he took him upstairs and into the attic to see the superior construction. The usual tours did not include showing tourists the attic.

Finally, the man took us outside to see the shacks where the former slaves had lived so long ago, both men and women. Some women worked in the fields.

We thanked the kind staff for the grand tour and headed to Lincoln's birthplace in Kentucky.

Lincoln's "Angel Mother."

After enjoying another scenic trip to Lincoln's birthplace, we located the small, one-room log cabin where he was born and spent his childhood. Guides showed us inside the now historic landmark through a door and we saw a small window. The door and window were the only light sources in the dimly lit room.

There was an enormous stone fireplace at one end of the room. The family used the fireplace for cooking and heating in the winter. The room became uncomfortably hot in the summer because it was the only way they had to cook. Candles and the fireplace were the only light at night.

Lincoln's birth mother died before he could remember her, and his father remarried. His new mother wanted him to be educated, but his father disagreed. His father would have Abraham gardening, cutting wood for the fireplace, and later cutting logs for his father to sell.

Still, his stepmother believed differently. She taught him to read and write at an early age. He did his studying late at night, by the fireplace light, after doing many other chores.

The guides told us how much Lincoln loved and appreciated his new mother. As an adult, they quoted Lincoln saying, "All I am or ever hope to be, I owe to my Angel Mother."

Lincoln in Springfield.

Bill and I decided to follow Lincoln's move to Springfield, Illinois, and took that scenic drive next.

Wanting to further his education as a teenager, Lincoln decided to move there where he would have better opportunities. It may have helped that he was six foot four inches tall, about a foot taller than the average man as a teenager.

Because he could read, uncommon for many men then, he secured a job as a clerk in a country store. He also earned extra money cutting railroad ties, a valued skill. He continued to study and became a well-educated man and an attorney.

During this time, he married a prominent young woman, Mary Todd, started a family, and they settled into a small cottage home in Springfield. He became interested and involved in local and state politics.

Where's My House?

The guides told us an interesting story about Lincoln in Springfield. A few years after becoming an attorney, he started doing horseback riding circuits once a year to provide legal services to people who did not have access to them. With each circuit, he was gone about two months.

One day he returned from a two-month trip. When he looked for his house, he could not find it. He checked with a neighbor. The man told Lincoln that his wife had a second story added to their house while he was gone, and Lincoln didn't recognize his home.

The former house had three bedrooms; now, there were seven. Even though the way Mary had accomplished the addition may have been questionable, the change was a good choice for their future.

Lincoln became increasingly more involved in politics. His wife proved to be an excellent hostess for his political friends, who often visited and stayed overnight. Mary had a live-in maid to help her with their children and do additional tasks.

Lincoln enjoyed having house guests. He didn't drink alcoholic beverages, nor did he serve them to his guests. But he became known for his deep well with icy cold water. Instead of serving alcoholic beverages, he served freshly drawn, icy cold water. They especially appreciated it in the hot summer when no ice was available.

Over the years, I had read extensively about all our presidents. My pleasure in visiting their homes was learning their human-interest stories about them. For a couple of

days, we also toured museums. There was a realistic statue of Lincoln that looked like he could start speaking at any moment.

Lincoln was known as a common man who cared about people and loved his country. Those are the main reasons they elected him president. I consider him our best president ever. At the very least, one of the best presidents of the United States of America.

It was time to head home. On the way, we traveled through more amazing scenery like I had never seen before. Every part of our country is beautiful in its own way. Nothing compares, though, with being back home again.

Chapter Five
THE BUSY YEAR CONTINUES

Easter and Family.

Bill and I arrived back home at Lake Waltanna before Easter. Settling in, we were ready to begin the many tasks awaiting us. First, Bill filled the squirrels' feeders with their favorite peanuts in cracked shells. The excited squirrels scampered around on the ground and "chirped" in the nearby trees. When he put the peanuts out for them, they jumped up on the pool fence and sat there, shelling and eating their treats.

Next came lawn chores. The new grass for the year was already growing. Bill hurried and mowed the church lawn so the kids could have their Easter egg hunt in the nice yard. He then mowed our lawn so our younger grandkids and great-grandkids could enjoy their Easter egg hunt later at our house.

Bill's chores continued. Another big one was taking care of the extensive process of uncovering, vacuuming, and cleaning the swimming pool. It was still a little cool to swim, but who knows? Someone might want to push the limits and jump in on Easter Sunday, as my brothers had done on the farm. If so, he wanted the pool ready.

Our church had its Easter Sunrise Services and the usual Sunday sermon. After church Bill and I hurried home for our family Easter dinner. We were increasing in size and numbers. There were now five grandkids old enough to drive. In addition, there were now six great-grandkids. We invited all to our Easter day dinner, but some couldn't be there. The wonderful smells of our usual large ham and many other festive foods and delicious desserts filled the air when they arrived.

After setting the food out on the table in our family room, buffet style, we held hands and asked for a blessing. Bill carved the succulent ham, and we feasted, off and on, all afternoon between Easter egg hunts.

Summertime.

Often unannounced, some of our grandkids who could drive sometimes came out to visit with friends that summer to go swimming in our pool. They knew Papa Bill would have snacks or meals ready for them. Sometimes he worked on their cars. He also spent time showing the grandkids, both boys and girls, the basics of car care.

I focused on caring for my flower beds and set out new plants until the beds were full. After a hard day working in the gardens, I jumped into the pool and swam laps or just relaxed and floated on my back. When I got out of the pool, there was always the temptation to turn on my hot sauna bath and relax some more, which I often did. Bill tried to ignore me.

Our lives were not just about caring for our home and doing various chores. Bill and I were active in our church. We invited families and individuals to visit us and swim in our pool. They knew we would have snacks, including the popular apples and little oranges that disappeared fast. In late summer, we had another Sunday evening, potluck dinner, and pool party for the church and visitors, with over one hundred guests to our home.

When it was too hot to work comfortably outside, we always found something to do inside. I spent time altering and mending our clothes as needed. I also liked to go to the fabric shop and usually found fabric and a pattern to make a new garment. Besides knitting and hand quilting, I did some cooking and cleaning. Bill cooked, cleaned, and did laundry. He was also good at relaxing and watching TV.

Green Ridge Reunions.

The former students from my Green Ridge country school started having reunions every other year, on the even years. This was the year, and it was held on the Saturday morning of the El Dorado Springs Picnic, the third weekend of July.

My family moved from the farm in 1941. The school closed in 1942 because there were not enough students to afford a teacher. I guess moving our family's five kids was the reason. They bussed the remaining students to larger schools. But the students who attended the school kept in touch.

I recall they held our first school reunion in the mid -1970s. Several students still lived in the area, but many of us had moved throughout the states. Local students planned for us to gather on Saturday morning in Jerico Springs, a small town south of El Dorado Springs, Missouri.

It was an exciting reunion, with over thirty former students attending. We each took turns "reintroducing" ourselves because some hadn't seen the others since we were small children. We talked about our life and answered questions from the others. Many of our spouses and kids were in attendance, and some listened intently, some not so much.

The aroma of the buffet dinner the local women's organization was preparing wafted through the meeting. They served a buffet of meats, main dishes, salads, cakes, pies, and other desserts. The home-cooked food was wonderful and greatly appreciated. Most of us returned for second helpings. By early afternoon, the former students gathered for group pictures.

The time came to head back to the El Dorado Springs Picnic. Bill and I walked around, visiting with our families who still lived there or came a distance to the picnic. Country bands and folk music were playing in the open-air pavilion. During the long evening, we snacked at the food stands.

It had been a long and exciting day. Bill and I headed back to our motel room for a good night's rest. One more successful trip. We ate at a local restaurant in the morning and headed back home to Lake Waltanna, where we could always rest the best.

Destination: Gettysburg.

Summer was almost gone, and it was time to think and plan for our fall trip. A niece and her husband had asked Bill and me to plan on attending their daughter's wedding in

Kansas City that fall, and the wedding would fit in with my plans.

After hearing about the Gettysburg Battlefield in Pennsylvania years before, I had always wanted to visit it and drive on to historic Philadelphia. I mentioned the idea to Bill, and he was eager to take the long drive. It would be a pleasure to see the variety of scenery in the five states we would pass through. It was a lot of driving, but Bill seemed willing for it.

We headed out one fall Saturday morning, dressed in our "Sunday Best," and attended the formal wedding in Kansas City. After attending the reception, we slipped out early to hit the road until late in the evening. Both of us were ready to spend the night in a motel and shed our dress clothes.

As we got on the road again, I noticed how Bill seemed relaxed and in his element the next morning. He loved to drive, and I was pleased to see how he enjoyed the trip as much as I was. The landscape was ever-changing, with unique fall colors in reds, golds, and greens. We stopped for meals and two nights in a motel on our way to Gettysburg, where I had a motel room reserved for our time there.

After breakfast the following day, we connected with tour guides and began our tour. Having read a lot about the Battle of Gettysburg, I thought it prepared me for the tour, and it had not. They gave us many gruesome details while driving us over the large, flat battlefield of many acres.

They fought the Battle of Gettysburg on July 1-3, 1963, between the Union Army and the Confederate Army. Believing he would win, General Robert E. Lee brought his

Confederate Army cavalry and ground troops to fight the Union Army, led by Major General George Meade. Each side had over 3,000 marching soldiers. And together, the armies had about 100,000 soldiers riding horse back.

After three days, the Confederate Army backed out in defeat. They lost over 4,000 soldiers in death, plus 12,000 soldiers in casualties. The Union Army lost over 3,000 soldiers in death and had 15,000 soldiers in casualties. Add to that, about 38,000 horses died.

The guides told us about the gruesome details. After the battle was over, dead bodies of soldiers and horses covered the several acres of fields. One could walk the length of the battle line without stepping on the ground.

We were told that the stream we saw running through the battlefield ran red with blood for over a day after the fighting ended. It took days for the soldiers' bodies to be removed and buried, many in unmarked graves. The stench was so foul that most of the 2,500 residents of Gettysburg left town for many days.

The traumatic tour took a couple of hours. I hope to never have to experience anything like the Gettysburg Battlefield again. But, as traumatic as the experience was, I'm glad I did the tour, and I'm not sure Bill felt the same way.

We were both tired and emotionally exhausted after the tour. Still, we ate a light supper before returning to our motel room. Bill was quieter than usual. Retiring early, we spent a restless night. I later realized that the tour may have brought back memories of his traumatic combat experiences when he was a soldier in World War II.

Nothing Is Better Than Home.

Early the following day, we got up, dressed for the day, and went out for breakfast. While eating, Bill quietly asked, "Would you be really disappointed if we didn't go to Philadelphia?"

We had planned to leave Gettysburg for Philadelphia that day. Realizing his possible trauma from the tour, I said, "Not at all. What do you want to do?"

After a moment, Bill answered. "It's a nice drive heading south from here. We would go through West Virginia, Kentucky, Northern Arkansas, and back home."

That sounded good to me, and I agreed to the change in plan.

Along the way, we stopped in Eureka Springs, Arkansas. We stayed in an old, restored historic hotel for a couple of nights. The stage shows of folk and gospel music were relaxing for us. But we were both ready to move on up the road, through the beautiful fall Ozark scenery, and head home.

Our trips were often amazing first-time experiences for me. Nothing was as good as being back in the comfort of our home and having our kids, grandkids, and great-grandkids around us and close by.

Ending the Year.

The holidays were more exciting than ever before, with our family growing bigger. We gathered once again for our Thanksgiving dinner with turkey and all the trimmings.

We ate and ate and ate some more. And we laughed and had a great time being together.

Then, after relaxing for a few days, Bill and I grew excited about the upcoming Christmas holiday. We unpacked our beautiful forever Christmas tree, turned on the lights, and decorated it. Sitting by the fireplace, we snacked and watched the upcoming holiday TV programs in our traditional way.

Bill and I took several trips to the mall to do our Christmas shopping. He sat at a table in the food court while I brought the gifts to him to watch. After a couple of hours, we ordered the food specialties we liked and enjoyed sitting there watching the other shoppers before returning home.

With new little ones being added to our family, our Christmas dinner get-together topped all our former Christmases. The dinner was better because some family members brought their special dishes and goodies. We were all together celebrating the weekend before Christmas, with Charlie and his family there from Oklahoma City.

Bill and I spent a quiet Christmas Day, watching TV and enjoying the "leftovers" from our family Christmas celebration. We reminisced about all the blessings of the past year for our family. And Bill and I were looking forward to a great New Year.

Chapter 6
New Year, More Travels

I Could Still Do It.

2001 looked like another busy year.

I had retired from school nursing and started drawing my Social Security. Several times, different people said to me, "You used to be a nurse." Attempting to not show my annoyance, I answered, "Not 'used to be a nurse,' I *am* a nurse."

This was the year for me to renew my Kansas State Nurses license, and renewal was due by the end of March, my birth month.

I took Continuing Education Units (CEUs) classes to renew my Nurse Practitioner License, which required thirty hours at the master's level. I attended some classes, but I preferred doing independent study at home with textbooks to study from. Then I mailed in the test for my passing grade. I learned more this way and had the textbooks for later reference.

The Nurse Practitioner License requires a large portion of pharmacology, which it should. I didn't know whether I would ever use the license professionally. At seventy years old/young, I just wanted to be able to say and show everyone I could still do it.

While feeling I would, I was still anxious until I heard

for sure the results. After a few weeks, they notified me I had passed the tests, and I received my Kansas license for another two years. Now I could finally relax, and so could Bill.

Let's Do It!

It was still late winter, and Bill and I spent long evenings watching our favorite TV programs. But I felt we were thinking the same thing: "Where were we going to take our spring trip?" The trip we took before it was time for Bill to open the swimming pool and mow lawns.

Then one evening, Bill quietly remarked, "We haven't been to Mountain View for a long time."

I exclaimed, "Let's do it!"

In the early 1970s, our son John was married and in his own home. He knew we liked folk music. He brought us a seventy-eight-style record of folk music from Mountain View, Arkansas, for Christmas. The music included guitars, banjos, fiddles, accordions, dulcimers, and harmonicas. We also received information about the town and its annual spring and fall festivals.

Bill and I decided to go to the Mountain View annual Spring Festival. It was a four-hundred-mile drive through the beautiful Ozarks. We didn't take our camper the first time because we would just explore the festival.

A Special Purchase.

Because there were no motels available there, we stayed in a motel in a nearby small town. When Bill and I arrived in Mountain View the next day, what we saw pleased us. Groups were singing, playing many kinds of instruments, and dancing around the courthouse square in the center of town.

We walked around the square and listened to the different groups who sang many gospel songs. And there was no need for anyone to be hungry. Many booths were offering local foods. So, we feasted off and on all day before returning to our motel room, full and tired.

Bill and I were so impressed with the spring celebration that we came back for the Fall Festival. We reserved a camper site ahead of time and brought our camper to stay for several days.

Again, when we got to the square in the mornings, we found the groups gathered, playing, and singing. They were still going strong when we reluctantly retired for the night.

One day, we noticed the Folk Center operated by the Arkansas Park Board. It was a couple of miles north of Mountain View, with the center laid out and enclosed on several acres. The outdoor covered stages had groups performing their recordings for all to see and hear.

The large, enclosed auditorium and stage were open in the evenings for an audience. While the musicians played and sang, square dancers and cloggers moved onto the stage and into the aisles. Anyone could join them as they chose, and Bill and I did not.

Throughout the grounds, there were booths of artists and craftsmen. I approached one quilter who was working on a quilt in a frame. I asked her what she would sell it for. She said, "$450.00." I told her I would like to buy the quilt, and she agreed to mail it to me when she finished it. To my delight, the beautiful quilt arrived about a month later.

A Mardi Gras Reenactment.

At one spring festival we attended, there was a reenactment of Mardi Gras. But it was like they did it in the rural areas of Louisiana. They did not allow drinking at the Folk Center. Chickens and small animals ran loose on the grounds. Dancers in colorful costumes seemed to be everywhere. Of course, there was Cajun music.

Bill and I walked down the sidewalk, enjoying the festivities. A young woman came up to Bill, drew him to her, and started swinging and dancing down the sidewalk. Surprised, he got into the dance for a minute or two. Then she danced away to someone else.

For many years before I started nursing in schools, we attended both spring and fall festivals. Mountain View became our favorite vacation place. As a school nurse, we could no longer vacation during the spring or fall when school was in session

Now that I had retired, we started attending both festivals most years. We decided to reserve a motel room in Mountain View several months before the celebrations instead of taking our camper. This freed Bill from the tasks of pulling, parking, and unhitching our camper.

We both enjoyed staying in the motel room, and they had a continental breakfast at no extra charge. When we got up in the morning, I dressed and went down to the breakfast bar and filled plates on a tray, adding coffee and orange juice. Since our room was close to the square, we could eat and hear the beautiful folk music playing around the courthouse.

After eating, we went down and joined the crowd once again.

Chapter Seven
THE YEAR ROLLS ON

Going For It Again.

It was good to be home after our spring trip and the family reunion in July. We restocked our fridge and freezer and spent time making our specialties for frequent visitors. Bill cleaned the pool and mowed lawns while I cleaned the house. I liked using the built-in central vacuum cleaner for our wall-to-wall carpet. The vacuum cleaner unit had long, expanding tubing which reached throughout the house. This was much easier than dragging a vacuum around and plugging it in again all the time.

My women's church group made weekly visits to a local nursing home. Some of the residents were church members. While there, we sought out other lonely residents with no family to visit them. Some of the kids from our church came in groups to sing and visit with the residents. Our visits were welcomed and enjoyed by all.

The Director of Nursing (DON) was a young RN. She was in a DON position for the first time in her nursing practice. She had been in the position for over two years and had not taken a vacation. She seemed surprised when I told her I was still licensed "at my age." As we talked, I told her of my previous work as a DON in long-term care.

As was common in nursing homes, there was usually

a shortage of nurses. After a few visits by our women's group, the DON asked if I would be interested in working part-time. Then, after orientation, I could work in the DON position so she could take a vacation.

Before I told her "Yes," I talked it over with Bill. As usual, he smiled and said, "Go for it!" He probably knew I was going to "Go for it" anyway.

After hiring on, I did a two-week orientation. I became acquainted with the staff: nursing, dietary, housekeeping, and maintenance workers.

The DON took her much-needed, much deserved two-week vacation while I served as DON. I'll admit, it was good to be back "in charge" again. All went well, but I realized I didn't want to work full time all the time... just when I chose. Later, I filled in occasionally when one of the nurses called in sick... and when I wasn't traveling.

Nature Causes a Change.

As we often did, Bill and I settled in one evening to watch TV when it started to rain. At first, gently, then powerfully with lightning and booming thunder. On the ten-o'clock news, the weatherman was predicting continued heavy rain. We felt safe in our sturdy brick home despite the weather, so we retired for the night.

The following day the rain had stopped. While Bill shaved, I dressed and went to the kitchen to start breakfast. I looked out the kitchen window over the sink, shocked by what I saw. I yelled for Bill to come and look. We stood looking out the window together, both feeling devastated.

One wall of our concrete swimming pool had collapsed, and half the pool water had drained away. We rushed outside to get a closer look at the damage. Our pool was old with poured concrete walls and bottom, and newer pools had a metal or thick plastic insert lining.

After talking to a professional, we were told to save the pool, we would need to have the concrete removed and have a new plastic or metal lining inserted in its place. The estimated cost of over $10,000 was prohibitive. We decided to have a contractor bury the concrete and fill it in with dirt where the pool had been. The work cost over $5,000, but we felt we had no other choice.

When we bought our home, we didn't think the pool could be saved. The realtor also considered the pool a negative, with a reduced price for the sale. It had not been cared for in years and was overgrown with blue-green algae.

At that time, Bill had come to the rescue. He didn't swim, but when we moved there, he cleaned the pool up and kept the pool going for us for over thirteen years. He never said so, but I'm not so sure that he wasn't relieved to not have to care for the pool any longer.

Back to Work.

While Bill supervised the filling in of our pool that August, I heard again from the last DON I had worked for. She asked if I would come to discuss future plans for the nursing home. She asked if I would be willing to meet with her and the other department heads, and the administrator. They wanted guidance and supervision in preparing for the upcoming Kansas State Nursing Home Survey.

The DON and the administrator offered me a part-time position as Staff Development Coordinator. They had learned of my prior work in nursing homes for having successful state surveys. When I talked with Bill, he said, again smiling, "Go for it!"

Taking a Stand on Smoking.

When I had served there as DON, I noticed how many of the staff took frequent and extended breaks to smoke, sometimes without reporting off. While they were out, the non-smokers had to pick up the slack in caring for the residents. It was a significant problem that needed to be addressed, and I had done it before.

When orienting for the Staff Development position, I met with the department heads and administrator. I mentioned my smoking concerns and suggested that we begin a stop-smoking in-service practice and positively address the issue before starting the Staff Development Program. I came to realize that some of the department heads were also smokers.

I explained that there were free resources from health departments to help our staff reduce and/or stop smoking, including nicotine gum, patches, and lozenges. I had previously used the plan in other facilities with some success.

The department heads were also concerned with the smoking issue, the loss of time for patient care, and how the issue would impact the upcoming state survey. It also puts an unfair burden on non-smokers. Even though some department heads smoked, they all somewhat reluctantly agreed to start the program.

Before starting our meetings, we held a meeting for all the staff. We reminded them of the time limits on breaks and the rules which required them to report to their supervisor before taking their break. The rules applied to all the departments.

After obtaining the needed stop-smoking supplies, we started mandatory weekly meetings for smokers. We met for a half-hour on Monday, between the first and second shifts. The non-smokers "took up the slack" for our meeting. They were used to covering for smokers and hoped to see positive results.

We kept the meetings encouraging. I explained how to use the products and how they could order their own. They were allowed to use the nicotine gum and lozenges while working. After a few weeks, the plan was beginning to work. Most of the heavy smokers reduced their number of cigarettes, and a few light smokers were able to quit.

Success Stories.

One of the greatest success stories was the Maintenance Department supervisor. He was approaching retirement and had smoked most of his adult years. He quit smoking with continued use of patches and lozenges and was working to eventually be free of nicotine. Nicotine is dangerous to health, only in the smoke of cigarettes.

Another success story was a maintenance worker, a young man who had a twelve-year-old son. The man had been rolling a week's supply of his cigarettes in packs. His son wanted his dad to quit smoking, so he convinced his dad to let him take over the task of rolling his cigarettes. Each week he rolled two fewer cigarettes in each of the week's packs.

It took several weeks, but the man, with the help of the nicotine products, was able to break the smoking habit. He brought his excited son to our meeting one day, and we celebrated their success. The man was proud of his son and pleased to be free of smoking. He and his son were an inspiration for other smokers to quit. Our stop-smoking program positively impacted both our employees and their families.

We considered the program successful, although a few smokers chose not to quit. They were, however, required to follow the rules for taking their breaks and were allowed no more break time than non-smokers.

History of Smoking in Nursing.

Sadly, there is a long history of smoking in nursing. When I started nursing school in the 'mid-70s at WSU, students walked the halls with lit cigarettes and smoked in the break rooms. Students sat on the floor in groups in the halls, studying and smoking.

Looking back, when I started into nursing practice in hospitals, the unit secretary could have a lit cigarette at the front desk where they greeted visitors. The long, narrow room where nurses did their charting had a counter with chairs, and their lit cigarettes filled the room with smoke. I chose another place to do my charting due to the dangerous secondhand smoke.

After a few years, however, the hospitals' regulations only allowed their staff to smoke outside the building. Eventually, visitors and patients were not allowed to smoke inside the hospital. However, it took longer for some nursing homes to enforce such rules. That's where I had some success with stop-smoking programs.

When I went back to WSU for my master's degree in nursing, the school policy changed. Smoking was not allowed in any of the buildings on campus. Smokers were required to go outside to smoke in all kinds of weather, a much-needed improvement for non-smokers.

A Man Called "Red."

In my Staff Development Coordinator position, I provided a thorough orientation to both new and present employees and monthly in-service programs to coordinate and improve resident care. I also helped pass out meds and helped serve lunch trays to residents either in their room or in the dining room. It was a good time to get to know both the residents and staff.

A young woman in our church began making weekly visits to the nursing home. Her grandfather had Alzheimer's Disease, but they did not want to put him in a nursing home. Her family members were working together to care for him. Her fourteen-year-old son was left to care for his grandpa for a couple of hours after school, and he enjoyed it.

One day, while he was caring for his grandpa, the old man slipped out of the house and ran away. The family and others spent several hours looking for him before finding him safe and sound. The grandson was traumatized and devastated, concerned with what tragedy could have happened. The man's daughter did not want to risk such disaster again and decided to admit him to our nursing home on a "trial basis."

The man, called Red, was outgoing and liked being around other people. His family visited him daily. On Saturday, after Red came to us, his daughter came to take him out to lunch. He countered when she told him what she planned to do, "I don't know why. The food here is perfectly good." She decided to stay and have lunch with her dad and us.

Sometimes Red was not cooperative with the staff when they got him up in the morning. One morning he came walking down the hall, quite upset, and I asked him what was wrong.

He looked at me and loudly said, "I don't like all this BS that's going on."

With humor, I responded, "Red, what if your daughter heard you say that?"

Smiling, he asked, "What's wrong with that? BS just means 'Baby Shoes.'" And he moved on to the dining room for breakfast.

Tough Adjustments.

I was thankful that I was there one day when Red's daughter and her husband came in carrying a suitcase. Some families did the laundry for their residents. When I said, "I didn't know that you do Red's laundry." She responded, "We don't. I'm here to take dad home."

I was deeply concerned. I asked Red's family to come into the quiet room and talk with me.

We sat down, and I asked her husband if he thought his wife should take her dad home to live. He quickly and firmly said, "No!"

I suggested that she wait a few more weeks before deciding to take him home. I knew it usually takes a couple of months for the resident to adjust to admission to a nursing home. Sometimes the family also needs time to adjust. She decided not to take him home that day.

It's possible that if I had not been there, she would have taken him home. She did adjust, and Red remained in our home for the rest of his life. Later his Alzheimer's advanced, and he eventually became bedridden.

One day Red's daughter asked to speak with me in the quiet room. She tearfully told me, "I want you to know I am grateful and thankful for Dad's care while living here, especially the nurse aides. Please let the staff know and thank them for me." Red passed a short time later.

A Sight to See.

One of our staff was a Certified Med Aide (CMA). Virgil finished his training, then took and passed the CMA class. He was middle-aged and rode a large motorcycle to work. Even though he owned rental property, he enjoyed being around the residents. He had a robust laugh, and the residents loved having him there.

During afternoon activity programs, Virgil liked dressing in special costumes. One of his and our favorites was him dressing as Santa Claus for Christmas. He was a large man and needed no extra padding, and he really looked and acted the part with a hearty "Ho Ho" laugh.

Halloween was coming up, and many of the staff and residents planned to wear costumes for our celebration. I was not. Virgil was a kidder. When I asked him what he would be, he laughed and said, "A ballerina!"

I thought, "A man that size, a ballerina? No way!"

On the afternoon of our Halloween party, we took our residents into the dining room. I saw Virgil slip into the men's restroom.

He was dressed in a glittering pink ballerina costume when he came out. It had narrow straps on the top with his hairy chest and arms showing. The costume had a fluffy tutu skirt and a glistening tiara. He wore ballerina slippers, and his tall and heavy body was a sight to see. Whenever I saw him throughout the afternoon, I couldn't stop laughing.

Checking in With Relatives.

Even though I was busy at work, Bill and I were both ready and anxious to be "on the road again" when mowing time was over for the year. We had never been to Mountain View during the nationally recognized Bluegrass Festival in mid-November. So, I made reservations with our favorite hotel with their continental breakfast ahead of time.

We hadn't seen Bill's siblings and his bachelor Uncle Carl for a while, so we left several days early to spend time with them. Bill felt at home there. He spent his early childhood on an adjoining farm and spent a lot of time with his grandparents, Uncle Carl's parents. Bill and Uncle Carl visited about "old times."

Uncle Carl liked that I could cook on his wood-burning cookstove. I made fresh apple pies and candied sweet potatoes, knowing he especially liked them. I knew he liked and expected me to make sausage gravy and homemade biscuits for breakfast. It was fun to cook on a wood-burning stove once again. But I was glad I didn't have to cook that way all the time.

After a few days, we moved on to Jefferson City to visit with Bill's siblings and their families. He had two brothers and two sisters who lived in the area. We stayed there for several days, then headed to Mountain View for the Bluegrass Festival, held in the Folk Center outside of town.

Enjoying Another Festival.

During the day at the festival, recording artists were performing on open stages throughout the center. Bluegrass music and songs were not my favorites, but they sometimes did gospel songs. We often heard a group singing "Amazing Grace," and the listeners would usually join in singing.

We didn't have a chance to get hungry. Food stands served ham and beans, meats, and candied sweet potatoes, to name a few items. The delicious aromas of barbequed meats prepared by local restaurants drew us. And there was a great variety of breads, pies, and other pastries from local bakeries. Bill and I sat in front of open stages with plates piled high, eating our fill… and more.

We moved to the theater when evening came, where

they played Bluegrass music for several hours. Tired and pleasantly exhausted, we headed back to our motel room for a good night's sleep. I would get our complimentary breakfast in the morning before heading back to the Folk Center.

The Year Draws to An End.

After several days there, we were ready to head back home for our family Thanksgiving get-together the weekend before Thanksgiving. We were all together and stuffed ourselves with turkey and more food than we could finish off. Just the way we liked it. I didn't think it was possible, but our family Thanksgiving get-together was better than ever before.

Christmas, too, was handled in our traditional way. We put up our permanent Christmas tree, shopped and ate at the mall before going home to wrap the gifts for our loved ones. Of course, there was another wonderful Christmas celebration with our growing family, and Christmas seemed to get better every year.

Before long, it was time to take down the Christmas tree for another year. Time to celebrate New Year's Eve and start planning for another year. If we were lucky… and blessed.

Chapter Eight
ANOTHER WONDERFUL YEAR

Pondering a Spring Trip.

For the fourteen years we had lived at Lake Waltanna, Bill enjoyed his two-mile walk around the lake before breakfast several times a week. "If the weather be good," as he said. He walked unless it was raining or snowing or severely cold or extremely hot, or we were traveling. I walked with him sometime, and I was not as determined to walk as Bill.

Over several years, I had wanted to visit two presidents' National Historic Landmark Homes: George Washington and Thomas Jefferson. Both were in the state of Virginia, about one hundred miles apart. But the distance there from our place was over a thousand miles.

One morning, while we were walking, Bill asked me where I wanted to go in the spring. When I mentioned the visit to the two presidents' homes, it didn't surprise him. We had discussed visiting their homes in the past years, but it had never worked out for us to take the trip. Bill was pleased and excited to take me there or wherever I wanted to go.

I had researched both Registered Landmark Homes, hoping to visit them someday. But they were so far away. Bill, however, didn't mind. And it just so happened that Mountain View was four hundred miles from us on the beautiful scenic drive to the presidents' homes.

Our Visit to Monticello.

We headed out and again stopped and enjoyed the Mountain View Spring Festival in early spring. It seemed to get better each year. After a few days there, we moved on down the road. We took two days to drive the six-hundred miles to Monticello, President Jefferson's home in Virginia. I had reserved a motel room close by for our tour of his plantation the following day.

We were first given a general overview of President Jefferson's life, spanning from 1743 to 1826, eighty-three years. He was from a wealthy family, a college-educated man, and the principal author of our United States Constitution and our Declaration of Independence. He became the third president of the United States from 1801 to 1809.

Thomas Jefferson was a proponent of democracy and believed that "All men are created equal." Nevertheless, he owned slaves, bred them, and sold them. He had owned over six hundred enslaved people during his lifetime. The ownership and selling of slaves were a major source of income for his plantation.

The slaves he kept cultivated the fields and gardens and planted and harvested the crops. They used some crops for both owners and slaves, and other crops were used to feed the animals: horses, cows, pigs, etc. The produce they grew helped make the plantation self-supporting and very profitable.

After the orientation, we took the guided riding tour of the main part of the vast plantation. There were crude cabins and kitchens for the field hands by the barns. The housing for house slaves near the mansion was nice framework and well cared for.

As we toured the barns, the guide showed us where they recorded the births of field-hand slaves, just like the records of horses and cows to be sold later. They then sold the enslaved people like animals.

Jefferson's wife, Martha, had a young personal house slave, Sally Hemings, who lived in the mansion to be near Martha and help rear the children. Jefferson and Martha had six recorded births of their children. Sadly, Martha died at a fairly young age.

After Martha died, Sally continued to live in the mansion to care for Martha and Jefferson's children. During the 1990s, DNA testing revealed that Thomas Jefferson also fathered at least six children by Sally Hemings. The tests performed on some of Sally's descendants are scientifically reliable and show that Thomas Jefferson is the father.

They sent Jefferson on a government assignment to Paris, France, for a couple of years. He took Sally with him as his housemaid. When they came home, Sally was pregnant. She continued to live in the mansion and had several children. Jefferson died in 1926. They interred him and Martha in the family vault at Monticello.

This is not a complete history of Thomas Jefferson's life, but what I remember from our tour of his Registered Historic Landmark Home. There was "so much good" about Jefferson's contribution to our country. But also, so much "not so good" about the man that I had not known before. Bill and I were both glad we took the tour of his plantation and learned about Jefferson's life.

Our Visit to Mount Vernon.

By late afternoon, Bill and I headed up the road, a couple of hours drive to President George Washington's Mount Vernon home, also a Registered Historic Landmark. After checking into the motel room, we enjoyed dinner in a nice restaurant and had a restful night's sleep. In the morning, we hurried to breakfast, then to our tour of Mount Vernon.

When we joined the tour group, Bill and I found the others were as ready and excited as we were. Before the tour started, they gave us a brief preview of George Washington's life. He was born in 1732, the first child of Augustine and Mary Washington. Mount Vernon was owned by Washington's great-grandfather, and it was eventually passed down to George's older half-brother. When he was twenty-two, he leased the plantation from his brother.

At age twenty-seven, he married the widow Martha Curtis. She had two small children, and Washington fathered no children of his own. In 1961, at age twenty-nine, he inherited Mount Vernon from his deceased older brother.

In 1975, they appointed him Commander-in-Chief of the Continental Forces: General George Washington. He did not live at Mount Vernon for eight years, and Martha visited him at his military headquarters several times. When he resigned his commission in 1783, he returned to Mount Vernon to retire at sixty-one years. It was not to be.

Washington was elected and served as President of our country for eight years, from 1789 to 1797. While President, he returned home to Mount Vernon fifteen times. He sometimes held government meetings in the mansion with many great government officials and dignitaries. He died about two years later, at age sixty-three.

While touring the plantation, we learned slaves ran it when Washington leased it. A highly qualified man, an enslaved person, managed it, including the house slaves, yard slaves and field slaves. The plantation could not have functioned without them. Washington opposed slavery, but the slaves were part of his inheritance.

It was not reasonable, even possible, for Washington to free the slaves. If he had done so, there was no way they could live as free men and women in our country. They taught some of his slaves basic math and how to read and write, who then taught other slaves. Some of them were as well educated as the general public.

Many of the slaves became accomplished craftsmen such as shoe cobblers repairing shoes, a much-desired skill. Other slaves were skilled furniture makers, and many women were accomplished in different needlework crafts. Washington allowed both men and women the free time to make and sell their craft in the local marketplace. The slaves kept what they made and used it to replenish their supplies. This was an opportunity for them to learn business skills.

At the end of George Washington's life, they revered him for his contributions to the forming and planning of our country. He wanted to be known as a common man. But he became better known as "The Father of Our Country," our first president.

President George Washington and his wife, Martha, are interred at Mount Vernon in the old family vault.

Ending Our Unforgettable Trip.

At the end of our tour, we considered staying for another day. But we headed home in time for Bill to mow lawns and feed his squirrels. When we settled into our motel room that night, he asked me if I would like to take a northern route home. I had never been that way before, but Bill had traveled there when driving for his job.

We started out the following day, and I was excited to go where Bill suggested. He knew the best tourist attractions along the super-highways. On our leisurely trip, we traveled through the northern parts of West Virginia, Ohio, Indiana, Illinois, and Missouri. The scenery was different, but beautiful and interesting in its own way.

We took four days for our drive back to Lake Waltanna. It was an unforgettable trip that I shall always treasure. Nothing, though, compares and is as good as saying, "It's so good to be back home again."

Back With His Buddies.

Late one afternoon, soon after arriving back home from our trip, we noticed Bill's squirrels were waiting on the pool fence for him. He first filled the squirrels' empty peanut trays with crushed-shell peanuts from the supply he always kept on hand. They grabbed the peanuts, chattering as they sat on the fence, shelling and eating them.

Then Bill and I enjoyed sitting and relaxing in our lawn chairs, watching his squirrels. When they saw us, they scampered down and sat close by, chattering, and waiting for him to hand them treats, which he had close by. He gave them their treats, and they scurried back onto the fence and sat shelling and enjoying their peanuts. Bill was back with his "Buddies."

Doing What He Enjoyed.

Before it got too hot, we spent many evenings in our reclining chairs, sitting close to where the swimming pool used to be. One evening, I asked Bill if he missed the pool.

He quietly answered, "Only in a good way." He seemed pleased that he no longer had to care for the pool. I really missed the pool, but I didn't tell him that, and I'm sure he knew.

Bill now had more time to do his favorite thing: work on cars. It had been a passion for him ever since we met. He was self-taught and had acquired professional manuals and mechanics magazines to learn and know what to do. He had got the needed tools and kept my car and his pickup in top-notch working order. Because of Bill's abilities, we never bought a new car. We owned several like-new, "fancy cars," which we could not have afforded otherwise,

He regularly watched the newspapers for used car ads. Sometimes the cars were not running, Bill was good at bargaining and got some excellent buys. He soon had the cars repaired and in great running condition, at little or no cost, and to sell to others.

Papa Bill enjoyed working on our grown grandkids' cars, too. He taught them the basics of caring for their cars, both boys and girls. At our small church, he became known for his mechanical abilities. He serviced the cars of our young pastor and his wife. He always kept their cars in good shape, at no cost to them, and was pleased to do it.

Other church members, family, and friends brought their cars to Bill for routine service. He became so busy that he had to make appointments. He was glad to save them money, and he was doing what he liked to do best: work on cars.

Success At Work.

After our trip, it pleased me to learn that my part-time work at our nursing home as Staff Development Coordinator apparently proved successful. Since the first of the year, we have held monthly meetings, educating staff on quality care for our resident's benefit and preparing for the upcoming state survey.

While we were traveling, they conducted the Annual Kansas State Nursing Home Survey. Upon returning home, I inquired our DON about the results. She said there were only minor deficiencies that the staff quickly corrected, and the state surveyors approved.

Then the DON gave me my Annual Evaluation, and she offered me a raise, which I accepted.

Bill Slows Down.

I noticed Bill was slowing down, just a little. He was only taking his two-mile walk around the lake two or three times a week. It was hard for me to keep up with him when

I walked with him in the past. His legs were longer, and he was eleven inches taller than I was. He was reluctant to slow down, so I had to hurry to keep up with him. Now his steps were shorter and slower.

Bill made more frequent visits to his cardiologist for adjustments and increases in his medications and frequent lab work. They had also had recently diagnosed him with beginning kidney failure. But he wanted me to "keep it quiet." Family and friends were not aware of the changes.

We made our trips to his doctor in Wichita "fun trips." We shopped for personal items for ourselves, did our grocery shopping, and usually dined at a pleasant restaurant, a treat for us.

We had lived at Lake Waltanna for fourteen years; we weren't getting any younger. Sometimes a visiting family member or friend would ask us, "How long are you going to live out here?" Bill would quietly respond with a smile, "Until one of us goes out feet-first." Then we all laughed, understanding what he meant. After all, we were country folks.

One morning while we were walking, Bill was unusually quiet for a while. Then he said, "You know. I've been thinking. Maybe we should move back to Wichita."

I was stunned and speechless, really. We continued to walk as I thought about what Bill had just said. As he looked at me, I responded, "You're probably right, as usual." Walking hand in hand, we headed home.

Planning a Change.

We both may have taken on too much with our traveling and our church work. Bill's lawn mowing and working on cars were huge responsibilities, which he took seriously. And as I usually did, I may have become more involved with our nursing home… than I should have.

Bill and I always spent many exciting times with our kids, grandkids, and great-grandkids. We could spend more time with them if closer to them in town. And we had many old friends who we could get reacquainted with.

We were both looking forward to going back to a simpler life in town. But having moved many times in our life, we realized we had a tremendous task ahead of us to make that change. We decided to sell both our camper and motorboat in our plan to simplify while the summer market was good. They both sold quickly to friends.

When we told our families that we would move, the announcement surprised and pleased them. They said they had become concerned that we had taken on too much responsibility. They didn't express it, but they "had become concerned about our age."

Bill and I decided to wait until after the holidays to list our house with a realtor. We were selling our house, not our home. As always, we were taking our "home" with us.

We still had several months to get our plans organized and in place. Bill mowed both the two-acre church lawn and our two-acre lawn with his riding mower at the end of summer. After servicing it, he sold the mower to a friend, knowing he wouldn't need it in a small yard in town.

Our nursing home staff, residents, and their families welcomed me when I showed up. I gradually cut back on my time there, except for our monthly staff development meetings. The staff was now working together to care for our residents. I told our DON that Bill and I were moving back to town, and I would resign after Christmas.

Bill's Squirrels.

Even though the pool was no longer there, our family often visited, especially our grandkids, mainly to visit Bill's squirrels. Sitting in a dinette chair by the open door, they took turns holding a crushed shell peanut for the squirrels to grab and carry to a resting place on the fence.

Often there were several squirrels in the dinette room. Occasionally, a grandkid sat in the recliner in the family room. A squirrel would scamper over, take a peanut from the child's hand, and run outside to climb on the fence and eat the peanut.

Our Best Thanksgiving Ever... Again.

The best part about our Thanksgiving and Christmas was, "They just got better each year."

I arranged for a neighbor to roast a small piglet for us, and it turned out delicious. The skin, though, was black. Bill skinned the piglet as he sliced it. The meat was tasty, but there was a lot left over. He packed and froze it in our freezer for later meals.

I made a roast turkey with rice stuffing for Thanksgiving

dinner, as I had done many times. This was my tradition since our first Thanksgiving when Johnnie was a baby. Our kids and grandkids brought many favorite covered dishes and desserts.

Bonnie's Potatoes and Peas
My family really liked my covered dish of new potatoes and peas. I didn't make it often
I liked to use new potatoes no bigger than an inch. they were hard to find out of season.
To start, I cooked them until done (until they broke apart easily). It was a process I learned from Mom.
I drained the potatoes and covered them with milk and thickened it, adding salt and pepper to taste.
Then I added a sprinkle of sugar to bring out the flavor.
I baked them in covered dishes for an hour at 350 degrees and were redy to serve.
They were all eaten, always.

After our prayer of thanks, we served dinner buffet style. The little grandkids sat on the stairs and on the floor. Their choice. It was our best Thanksgiving ever. I seem to keep saying this, but every time I mean it.

And The Best Christmas Ever.

After Bill and I put up our "forever" Christmas tree and decorations, it was time to shop at the mall for our extended list of gifts for each one of our family. There were now three generations of us. They may not have expected gifts, but we wanted to give them, anyway.

We needed to rethink our gift-giving plan. Shopping was becoming more difficult. Even though I had asked most of our family members what they would like, it was difficult. I recalled asking our ten-year-old grandson what he would like for Christmas one year, and he shyly replied, "Anything but a sweater." We bought him a toy.

It was to be our last Christmas at Lake Waltanna. There were now twenty of us and I wanted to make this one very special. Colorfully wrapped presents were piled high under our Christmas tree, and we began opening them, starting with the youngest. Everyone "seemed" to be pleased with their gifts.

To start our family's unique Christmas celebration, a grandson read "The Night Before Christmas." Then we joined in singing Christmas carols, a cappello. Some sang parts and some sang off-key, but that was okay. You don't need perfection to enjoy the special time together. Bill didn't join in the singing, but he quietly played his harmonica. It was our family's unique Christmas celebration.

Meanwhile, some of us finished preparing for our fabulous dinner of ham and all the "fixin's," including the dishes and desserts our kids brought. After our prayer, we feasted and visited all day long, not feeling eager for the time together to end. Yes, it was our best Christmas at Waltanna... and our best family Christmas ever.

Santa's Best Performance.

The Activity Director at our nursing home planned a Christmas party for both residents and staff. We gathered in the main dining room one afternoon. As we sang Christmas carols, we heard tinkling bells and a hardy "Ho ho ho!" loudly singing "Jingle Bells."

Suddenly Santa Claus (Vergil) came running into the room, fancy-stepping and greeting us. He had grown his beard long white, and fully filled out his suit with no need for extra padding.

Groups of entertainers continued to sing Christmas songs as it became "Santa time." Santa sat down and had each resident who could sit on his lap and tell him what they wanted for Christmas. Everyone enjoyed this fun time.

Then Santa went to the other residents to visit with them, including some who were bedfast. He went to their rooms and wished them Merry Christmas as we continued to sing. We could hear him singing "Jingle Bells" as he moved down the halls.

When Santa returned to our party, he read "The Night Before Christmas." With the poem's last words, "Merry Christmas to all and to all a good night," Santa left us as noisily as he came with a loud and hearty "Ho ho ho" and the ringing of his tinkling bells.

It was a day I shall never forget, the best Santa performance I have ever seen. Santa—Vergil—and I had become friends, and we exchanged phone numbers to be used later.

Anticipation.

It had been yet another incredible year in our home at Lake Waltanna. Bill and I and our growing family were all excited for us to be moving back to Wichita the following year. I was always optimistic; I anticipated the very best for Bill and me, and I think Bill did, too.

Chapter Nine
WICHITA HERE WE COME

Finding Our New Home.

With the holidays behind us and a new year ahead, Bill and I began thinking about looking for our "new home to be" in Wichita. First, we listed our property at Lake Waltanna with a realtor we worked with in the past, Jerry Self.

Over a couple of weeks, Jerry showed us several houses which he thought Bill and I might like, bur none of them "clicked" with us. One day he called saying a new listing had come on the market, and he thought it might be just what we were looking for. He wasn't the listing realtor for the house, but he wanted us to see it.

We met Jerry at the location on west 19th street. The house was a handsome, nearly new ranch type, sitting back from the road, with a two-car garage. Bill and I walked up the long walk with him to the front door and stepped inside.

The house was in perfect condition. Inside the front door was a stairway with ornate handrails leading to the lower level. The spacious living room had a huge, decorative picture window covering the opposite wall. I walked over to the side of the living room to the open door leading to the spacious dining-kitchen combo room.

The kitchen had many beautiful built-ins and a center island with a countertop work surface. A door by the cabinets led to the garage, and another door led to a hallway, two bedrooms, and a bathroom. Another large picture window and a door to a natural wood deck were by the spacious dining area. It was a lot to take in immediately.

I turned to Jerry and exclaimed, "We can't afford this!"

He quietly and calmly said, "I wouldn't have brought you here if I didn't think we could work something out for you and Bill." He could plainly see that I wanted the house. Oh, and Bill really liked what he saw, too.

Then he showed us the master bedroom, which had a large, ornate picture window covering the room's front wall. There was a lovely, padded window seat and a walk-in closet on each side of the doorway into the bathroom.

The three-quarter bathroom had a long vanity with two sinks, "one for each of us." There was only a shower, no bathtub. I knew Bill to say whimsically, "I haven't taken a bath in years." He took showers, and I often took showers too, but I could take baths in the other full bathroom.

We went downstairs to the fully carpeted family room and two bedrooms. Bill and I noticed a corner installment for a three-quarter bath without the fixtures. Still, all the plumbing connections needed for a sink, stool, and shower were there.

Back upstairs, we went through the kitchen door into the oversized two-car garage. A long, sturdy workbench across the inside wall was just what Bill "needed" to lay out his tools. We left hoping this house would be "the one for us."

Selling and Buying.

We listed our house in Waltanna with Jerry, who showed it often. One day, he showed the house to a middle-aged bachelor businessman who traveled a lot. He had been looking and hoping to buy a house at Waltanna. Many owners there passed their homes down to their families or sold them to someone they knew without listing them with a realtor.

The buyer wanted a house for his "headquarters" and a place to relax and fish on the lake. The fishing was excellent there. After looking through our house, he signed a contract for our asking price on the spot. And he was willing to wait until we bought and moved to the house we were buying.

The owners of the house we wanted on nineteenth street were inheriting a small fortune but had not yet received it. They had signed a contract for a vacant mansion but could not close until they sold their house. With Jerry's help and planning, we signed a contract for their house, our future home.

Jerry had a plan. One morning, all of us involved in the deals gathered in an office to sign the needed paperwork. The man buying our house had obtained his loan; we closed the deal, and he wrote us a check. They deposited the payment into Bill and my checking account.

Our realtor had negotiated for us, and the owners of the 19th street house had agreed to a reduced sum below their listing price. Bill and I and the owners signed the closing contract on "our home to be." We did not have to get a loan, and we could write a check for the total amount because the payment from our house in Waltanna covered the price of our new home and the realtor's fee.

The sellers had not yet received their inheritance, so they had to get a loan for their mansion, which they could now do by selling their house. They had been in a time-bind. Upon receiving our check, they closed on their purchase and immediately began moving.

The Chaos of Moving.

Our kids and grandkids helped when they could. With possession of our new home, Bill hired a mover for the big items. We were busy packing boxes of personal items to haul in his pickup, and he and our son John loaded the things in the garage onto John's two-wheel trailer.

One day the buyer of our house showed up. We invited him inside. He told us of some significant changes he was planning to make. I told him I made the window treatments throughout the house. He said, "Oh, you can take the curtains. I want a simpler look."

I was pleased. The draperies were valuable but would require major alterations to fit the windows in our new home. "But that's what I do!" We took all the window treatments down that day.

Excited to be moving back to Wichita, Bill's only regret was leaving his squirrels, his little "buddies." He had enjoyed them for fifteen years. He left a supply of crushed peanuts for the new owner to feed the squirrels, and Bill explained how he fed them.

A few days after finalizing the sales, the mover came,

loaded up our furniture, and headed for our new home. We were excited and pleased to be back in Wichita. And Bill was pleased to be mowing a much smaller lawn. There was no time or desire to take a trip that spring. We wanted to be right where we were.

Busy Settling into Our Home.

Bill and I were always busy, each with different tasks. He wanted to get the three-quarter bathroom downstairs functioning as soon as possible. He was anticipating the many guests, including our family, who would sleep downstairs. He didn't want them to have to come upstairs to the bathroom.

Within a few weeks, he had the sink, stool, and shower hooked up and functioning. Just in time for the flood of house guests that summer, to "Willie's Hotel."

I busied myself with outside tasks. The previous owner had run a daycare for preschool kids for many years. She had a large, eight-by-twelve-foot sandbox in one corner of the yard. The sides were about a foot high, with landscaping logs around it, filled to the top with sand. I thought it was a real eyesore. It had to go… with Bill's help.

This was quite a job for us. We filled five-gallon buckets with sand and loaded them in Bill's pickup to take to friends and family. Then he hauled off the logs. We then scattered buckets of sand in the flowerbeds where I had dug up the grass, and I transplanted the grass into the bare space where the sandbox had been.

I spaded flowerbeds by the front driveway and around the backyard fence, a few feet at a time. I dug a small area beside the back of our house for my vegetable garden. First, I planted the vegetable garden to ensure a good crop for the summer, and I bought tomato and sweet pepper plants to get an early start. There were short rows of radishes, leaf lettuce, carrots, etc. It was good to have fresh veggies at my fingertips again.

After starting the veggie garden, I visited a nursery. I purchased blooming flowers, both annuals, and perennials, which would be most colorful that spring and summer. At the same time, I ordered peonies and iris from mail-order catalogs to establish permanent flowerbeds. They would not bloom until next spring. But the roses I ordered from my catalog would bloom that spring and summer.

Bill was enjoying cooking in our new kitchen. As he worked at the island counter, he could look through the large kitchen window where there was a bird-bath fountain. While preparing his famous lasagna, beef stew, and many favored deserts, he watched the water spraying up as the birds sat singing and splashing in the fountain.

Bill and I had searched for a church close to our new home. We had friends in several churches who wanted us to join their congregation but chose a church close to us. We were welcomed and felt "at home," so we moved our membership there. We attended worship services and church dinners, but we didn't get involved in positions of responsibility.

Bill's "Addiction."

Bill preferred to do his grocery shopping twice a week, every Tuesday and Saturday, with or without me. When I went with him on those days, I noticed he always bought a lottery ticket, and he then checked to see if he had won anything on his previous ticket. Sometimes he won a small amount, but a few times, he won up to a hundred dollars.

I realized Bill had become addicted to gambling.... "Jus' Kiddin'." He bought a $2.00 lottery ticket each time he went to the grocery store. He knew I disapproved of gambling, so he hadn't mentioned his "addiction" to me. Actually, I was glad he was enjoying himself.

Our Lawn Chairs.

Every morning when Bill got up, he shaved and dressed for the day. He never lounged around in pajamas, housecoats, and slippers. He dressed in blue jeans, a western shirt, and engineer boots. But I usually stayed in my jammies, housecoat, and house shoes for a while.

Bill's birthday was in April. Susan dropped by often for a short visit. One day she brought her dad a deluxe, adjustable reclining lawn chair for his birthday. He set the chair up on our deck and relaxed, enjoying it. At times, when he was busy, I sat in his recliner, easily adjusting it to fit me.

One day I said to Bill, "I wonder where Susan got this chair. I'd like to get a matching one for me."

I spent the next morning at the nursery getting plants and supplies I needed and wanted. Bill wasn't interested in going with me. I returned home and walked into the kitchen to get something to drink.

Bill was working at the kitchen island. After a moment, he said, "Did you look out the back door?"

I walked over to the back door. When I looked, I saw not one but two matching lawn chairs sitting side by side on our wooden deck. Bill walked up behind me and softly said, "That chair is for our anniversary." Which is in May.

I turned and asked, "How did you know?"

With a mischievous smile, he said, "Well, you *whined around.*" His voice intentionally trailed off.

Bill and I spent many lovely evenings relaxing in our recliners over the next few years we had together. When Bill passed on, I gave his recliner back to Susan. But I still have the recliner he gave me, and I always will.

Wallpapering Once Again.

Word soon got around to my extended family about our new home back in Wichita. Several families lived around Springfield and Republic, Missouri; some had moved there from Colorado. When they wanted to go back to visit, it was too far for a one-day trip, and Wichita was a day's drive away for them. Bill and I liked they made our home an overnight or a few days' stop on their way. On their way home, they stopped again, much to our delight.

With summer coming, it got too hot to work outside all day with the flowers and veggie garden in good shape. I had lots of things I wanted to do inside. First, I altered the draperies from our former house to fit the picture windows in our new home.

As I mentioned before, the former owner of our house ran a daycare for preschool-age kids. She papered the two side bedrooms with kiddie-type wallpaper of animals and cartoons, turning the rooms into playrooms. Not the best look for our many guests.

One bedroom had a large picture window looking out onto our beautiful backyard. On the opposite wall, there was a closet with double doors. The room would double as my office and a bedroom with a sofa bed. I wanted a unique paper for the room.

I visited my favorite wallpaper store for the unique, appropriate designs. Wallpaper can be pricey, so I looked for the odds and ends of discounted bargains. After a long search, I came across a small bundle of gold lame paper, which had initially sold for over ten dollars a single roll. The bundle of four double rolls was now less than five dollars. I bought it!

Even if the paper only covered part of the room, I could finish it with another complementary paper. It didn't have a matching pattern. With careful maneuvering around the large picture window, the double-door closet, and the entry door, I papered the entire room.

Finally, I papered the other bedroom with nice, discounted paper, appropriate for a bedroom. Now our guests could sleep well, but I don't think they were bothered by the kiddie paper as much as I was.

Stepping Back to Remember Something.

A brief history. Well, maybe not so brief. When we lived in our Historic Landmark house on Park Place, descendants of a former owner shared family history and pictures with me. They told how their grandmother had a massive ornate fireplace removed from the front parlor on an inside wall.

Park Place house

She removed the wall between the two rooms to have one long family room. There was a fireplace in the other room on the outside wall. After a few years, she had to replace the wall she had removed because it was a supporting wall.

Her family told me their grandmother sold the fireplace to a wealthy local jeweler for a huge sum of money. He used it as the centerpiece of the new home he built. The family gave me the jeweler's name. I called and told him I would like to see the fireplace. I told him they had taken it from the home where we lived, and I wanted to duplicate it and replace it in our home.

The jeweler made an appointment with me to meet him at his home. He was an older man, and it had been several decades since he had his house built around the fireplace. He invited me inside his enormous brick mansion. As I looked around, it overwhelmed me with its beauty.

The massive, ornate fireplace sat against the front, outside wall. The parlor room had a vaulted, two-story ceiling. There was a hallway and handrails in front of the upstairs bedrooms, which looked down on the parlor. Back to the fireplace....

It was the most beautiful fireplace I had ever seen. There were inset beveled mirrors above the mantel and ornate turnings that supported the hooded top above the large, beveled mirror. I took pictures to give copies later to the craftsman I knew who could duplicate the fireplace.

Around the fireplace's firebox were beautiful, green-glazed ceramic tiles with lovely female figurines and flying birds molded on them. My first thought was, "I can do that." I had taken some art classes when I was at WSU and became acquainted with instructors.

I contacted a former instructor and told him what I was planning/hoping to do. I gave him pictures of the tile, and he made clay slabs the size I needed, allowing for shrinkage when fired. The top and side tiles were six by thirty-two inches, with two corner tiles six by six inches.

He brought the unfired tiles to my house on slabs of wood and laid them on our formal dining room table, along with a large wad of wet clay. I would use the clay to mold the figurines and flying birds on the slabs of clay... freestyle.

I worked full-time in nursing but found time to work with the clay figurines. In a couple of weeks, I called the art instructor to pick the finished tile up. He took them back to WSU, fired, and glazed them dark green.

When they were finished, he called and delivered the tile to me. There was no charge to me for the clay, the firing, or for the pickup and delivery. Now that the tile was finished, I could call the craftsman who could duplicate the fireplace for a complete restoration of the house.

My plan was for Bill and me to live out our life together

in our home on Park Place. As it turned out, it was not to be.

Bill suffered a heart attack and had to have bypass surgery. Thankfully, he recovered well but had to quit driving for JI Case. He was sixty-two. However, Bill had an excellent union disability retirement until he was sixty-eight, with an income over half of his former income.

But everything changed. Bill had very few limitations and wanted to buy a house on a small acreage in the country… me, not so much. I was willing to move, but not to a farm again. We were both pleased to find a house on two acres at the Lake Waltanna development.

It was time, maybe past time, for me to give up Park Place. Nevertheless, I treasured the fireplace tiles I made and stored them away until I could find a way to frame and display them. Once again, Bill came to the rescue….

We had decided to move back to Wichita in the spring. My birthday is on March 2nd. One day, Bill asked me what I wanted for my birthday, and I told him I wanted to have the tile I had made set in frames so we could hang them on the wall.

Bill made sturdy frames of plywood backing with a framework perfectly fitted around the tiles. But there was a problem: they were too heavy to hang. By now, it was getting time to focus on moving, so I set the framed tiles aside at the time.

A Treasured Project.

Bill was always good at thinking of new ideas, and he made a kitchen-dining area in our family room downstairs.

He placed our ornate, wrought-iron dinette table and matching chairs on one side of the room. Close by, he put a large microwave and a small refrigerator for snacks and drinks on a table in the corner. He always kept a supply of paper plates and cups for us.

We completed the cooking in our kitchen upstairs, carried the food downstairs, and set it up buffet-style on the table. There was a sofa, recliners, and chairs throughout the large room. The kids often sat on the stairs and in groups on the soft carpeted floor. We all enjoyed the relaxed and comfortable atmosphere, and Bill was glad his plan worked so well.

Many of our guests noticed the framed fireplace tiles leaning against a wall in the family room. One day, Bill suggested we secure them against the wall and add a narrow mantle to join them so they would look more like a fireplace.

After a few weeks, Bill and I together had built a foot-deep case behind the tiles and added a mantle to top it off. We set our now stand-alone fireplace against the wall. We searched for a realistic-looking flaming log fireplace insert with a metal frame and glass door. When John saw our completed project, he remarked about how pretty it was. This was the only fireplace in our new home.

I treasure that fireplace mainly because it is one of only a few projects and accomplishments which Bill and I worked on together. I now have the fireplace in my bedroom, and eventually it will be passed down to the family.

Our special fireplace

Completing Another Project.

Soon after we moved back to Wichita, Charlie and his family visited us from Oklahoma City. Our family room downstairs was almost complete. We hadn't installed the ceiling, and the exposed rustic ceiling framework was barely noticeable... but he noticed

Charlie was a union carpenter and worked for a drywall company. Installing ceiling grids and tiles was his line of work. His boss gave him surplus gridwork and ceiling tile left over from large jobs. And Charlie's labor was worth a fortune to us. We could not have afforded the eight-hundred square feet of supplies at full cost and labor.

So, Charlie came one weekend, bringing all the ceiling grids and tile. Bill helped as he could and watched Charlie work as he installed the grid. But there was more than Charlie could get done on one weekend, and he didn't have time to do one bedroom. He left the needed materials and said he would return and finish it.

Guess what? The following week, Bill decided he could and would hang the gridwork in the bedroom himself, which he did. Then I fitted the tile in place as I saw Charlie do it. Now our new home was complete.

Wrinkles.

Bill had been dealing with cataracts in both eyes for a couple of years, and knew he would eventually need to have them surgically removed. Finally, his optometrist said he couldn't put it off any longer. I went with Bill for his surgery on one eye, and I drove us back home. A few weeks later, he had the other cataract removed.

In a few weeks, Bill got his new glasses. One morning at breakfast, he was sitting in his captain's chair at the head of the table, and I was sitting close by. He had regained his eyesight and was reading the morning paper. We had finished breakfast and were both sipping our coffee, and he started talking about something he had read.

Still talking, he looked up at me. Suddenly, he said, "You've got wrinkles!"

He was really embarrassed, but I thought it was funny. "I'm going to take you back and have that surgery undone!" I said jokingly. He was seeing so well, and I was really pleased. I already knew I had wrinkles… now Bill knew I had wrinkles.

Relaxing and Dancing.

We had relaxing days when we didn't have guests. We sat together on our settee, ate lunch from our TV trays, and watched our favorite shows. Bill would usually doze off, unintentionally, I think. I would go to the kitchen and prepare favorite foods and desserts for our guests, and us.

I always had music on the radio or record player, usually our favorite country and folk tunes. One day, I was making cookies at the center kitchen counter. I looked up and Bill was standing at the kitchen door, fancy-stepping and snapping his fingers to the music. He waltzed over to me, pulled me into his arms, and we danced around the dining room, across the smooth wood-plank floor together. This happened more than once.

A Delicious Change.

We were too busy to take a road trip that fall. The holidays were fast approaching, and I was planning my grocery shopping list for our favorite foods for Thanksgiving. I knew Bill didn't especially like roasted turkey but didn't make a fuss because our family expected it.

As I was planning to buy our turkey, Bill said, "I heard about a store that sells smoked turkeys. Let's try one this year." I agreed, and he bought a large smoked turkey. I made the usual rice stuffing our family liked and expected.

At our Thanksgiving dinner, we gathered and offered our traditional prayer of thanks. The pleasant aroma filled the air when Bill carved his smoked turkey. It didn't seem possible, but our Thanksgiving that year was better than ever before, thanks to a smoked turkey.

Our grandson, Mark, was a teenager that year. Recently, he remarked about Papa's delicious smoked turkey that first year. He said it was much better than a roasted turkey.

The Holidays Keep Getting Better.

Taking a few days to recover from the Thanksgiving dinner, it was now time to get ready for Christmas. We put our forever Christmas tree in a corner of the downstairs family room. And we left the tree up year-round for as long as we were there. We decorated it and throughout our home, both upstairs and downstairs.

As was our habit for Christmas shopping, Bill and I went to the mall. He sat at a table in the food court as I shopped, then we ate lunch there. It took a couple of trips to complete the shopping list that grew longer each year.

We gathered the weekend before Christmas to celebrate, with Charlie and his family coming from Oklahoma City. We were all together Saturday evening, and everyone brought food for snacking throughout the evening. Our big Christmas dinner would be the next day, Sunday.

Bill was the only one who had been told that Santa (Virgil) would show up on Saturday night. I bought small gifts for the younger kids and put them in a bag with their names. I set the bag just outside the front door, prearranged by us. When Santa came, he set the toys in his bag, looking like he had brought them.

Santa rang the doorbell and came in laughing, hohohoing, and wishing us a Merry Christmas as he walked down the steps to where we were. An oversized rocking chair was close by for him. The little kids were so excited to have Santa at our house.

Santa doing his job.

Santa told the eager kids that he had toys for the boys and girls who had been good. Of course, they all claimed to be. He reached into his bag, pulled out a toy, and read the child's name. He asked the child to come and sit on his lap.

When they did, he talked and laughed with them, then gave the child their toy.

We had a great-granddaughter, Alyssa, who was just two years old. Santa called her name, and she slowly walked up to sit on his lap. He was laughing and bouncing her on his knee when she jumped down from his lap and ran to her Mommie.

Santa called another child's name and gave them their gift, and he gave out all gifts, except Alyssa's. We tried to persuade her to go back and get her gift, and she started trudging back to Santa as he reached out to her.

When she got close to Santa, she stopped, shook her finger at him, and firmly said, "No more laughing!"

It was difficult for Santa to stifle his laughter, but he did. He sat Alyssa on his lap and gave her gift to her as she smiled at him. It all ended well.

Santa and grandchildren

Santa lingered long enough to read "The Night Before Christmas" and sing Christmas carols with us before hustling up the stairs and out the front door into the night.

Sunday morning, we had our usual extensive gift exchange, besides what Santa brought. Then we gathered around the table, holding hands, and asked God to bless the food and our family, now and in the year to come.

Bill carved the ham, and we settled down to our fabulously festive Christmas dinner "with all the fixin's." Some of us sat at the table, but most grandkids filled their plates and sat wherever they wanted. With the desserts, our Christmas dinner lasted most of the afternoon.

Yes, it had been our best family Christmas ever and the end of another wonderful year. Have I said that before? Well, I meant it. Again.

Chapter Ten
THE YEARS AHEAD

Our Everyday Life.

With the holidays behind us, Bill and I could now relax or keep busy. We both spent time cooked and baked the favorites we knew our family and other guests liked. Our large freezer stored the foods for unexpected or expected company. And it happened often.

I decided to paper our kitchen-dining room, and I searched for a discounted paper at my favorite wallpaper store in a pattern I wanted for the room. The papering took several days to complete, and Bill liked the new look, too.

When we weren't entertaining guests, we watched our favorite TV programs. Sometimes Bill would bring out his harmonica and play, and he wanted me to get my guitar and accompany him. He played the old folk songs and hymns and always encouraged me to sing the songs I knew. And I knew most of them, if not all of them. Our favorites were "Amazing Grace," "Farther Along," "In the Garden," "I'll Fly Away," and "Rock of Ages."

There are benefits to having kids and grandkids. They insisted we leave the snow shoveling for them to do, and they always showed up promptly to shovel and swept our walk and driveway.

Mountain View Again.

Because Bill and I were so busy planning and moving back to Wichita, we had not taken a road trip for over a year. We were both looking forward to another trip to Mountain View for the spring festival and stopping on our way back. But Bill's older sister and his Uncle Carl had both passed away, and no more visits to his uncle's farm.

When we left in early spring, we took the scenic southern route to the annual festival in Mountain View. We enjoyed the scenery as much or more than ever. The beautiful redbud trees were blooming on the hillsides, along with flowering fruit trees, bushes, and wildflowers throughout the fields. Bill was glad to be "on the road again." So was I.

We left home early and stopped for lunch on our eight-hour drive to our destination. When we arrived, we checked into our favorite motel. The festival was in full swing around the courthouse. We snacked from the food booths on our favorites of sweet potato fries and Frecn fries made from locally grown potatoes. And we walked around as we listened to many local groups sing and play their instruments. We welcomed the chance to walk around after sitting all day.

Pleasantly exhausted, we retired for a restful night's sleep. The following day, as had become my habit, I went to the motel breakfast buffet and gathered delicious food. We enjoyed our breakfast in our room before starting our exciting day at the festival.

Bill and I moved from one group to another. Some families sang together, including their children. Family harmony was usually excellent. And they had a variety of folk and gospel, just what we liked best. Twenty or more groups sang simultaneously on the lawns and sidewalks but were far enough apart to not interfere with each other.

Across the streets, around three sides of the courthouse, were rows of stores. A variety of stores sold local quilting, other fine needlework, and homemade foods: soups, meats, and desserts. Some stores sold small, handcrafted wooden pieces made from beautiful walnut wood. We shopped and bought gifts we knew family members would like when we could afford them. They were reasonably priced, but more than we usually spent on gifts,

In the evening, we drove to the Folk Center close by to watch the performance of professional musicians on stage. Most were recording artists and had records and videos for sale. You guessed it; we bought some of each. Our kids and grandkids enjoyed them, as we did.

After four days and five nights, Bill and I headed back home. We planned to stop in Jefferson City to visit Bill's younger sister, his two brothers, and their families for a couple of days before heading home. I realized Bill wanted/needed the break on our trip, and I decided I would plan breaks on our future trips.

Jam-packed Summer.

It was "good to be back home again." As exciting and fun as our trips were, "there's no place like home" where we can relax and enjoy our many comforts of home.

We had a jam-packed and exciting summer. Some of our grandkids stayed with us for a few days throughout the summer. They wanted to keep busy, so the big ones helped Bill with the mowing. And they all liked to help me in my veggie garden, pulling weeds and picking tomatoes for slicing or just eating out of hand.

There was never a shortage of guests. Bill didn't enjoy being a guest in someone else's home but looked forward to our guests and serving them his "famous" foods. He had beef stew, lasagna, and other casseroles and desserts in the freezer, always ready for frequent company.

Bonnie's Fruit Salad
Our family always expected my fruit salad. It was my idea to provide a healthful choice for dessert. It was my unwritten recipe.

In a large bowl, I sliced a couple of bananas.
Next, I added dark grapes, fresh pineapple, chopped apples, strawberries, peaches, and any fruit that blended in.
After they were all mixed together, the juices seeped out and covered the fruit.

Our Fall Trip.

Bill and I took a road trip over four hundred miles to Mountain View, Arkansas, for over twenty years, and treasured each unique journey. We saw that many older people had moved there permanently, and we didn't want to do that. But we enjoyed one or two trips there each year.

So, yes, once again that fall, we took another road trip there. On our way, we stopped to visit my brothers and their families in Republic, in southern Missouri. We stayed and visited with them for a couple of days, then headed to our destination.

As we had before, we enjoyed our time together taking in the festival. We spent several exciting days and nights there before heading home. The weather was beautiful, and we made the trip last a leisurely two days. As always, it was good to be back home again.

Another Memorable Holiday Season.

Thanksgiving dinner was our usual yet unusual grand experience. There were now twenty-two of us. First, we gathered around the table, set up buffet-style, and asked for the blessing. As Bill carved our smoked turkey, we began loading our plates, kids first.

The kids went downstairs and sat throughout the large room. They may have known that we had set all the desserts on the dinette table down there. Grownups filled their plates and sat around the dining table upstairs. Soon we all went downstairs to where the desserts were.

We relaxed by our flickering fireplace and noisily visited while the kids played games. It was another exceptional family Thanksgiving Day and as good as they come.

After recovering from that holiday, Bill and I began putting Christmas decorations on our forever Christmas tree and throughout our house. Once again, we shopped at the mall for our family's gifts.

Continuing our family tradition, we met on the weekend before Christmas. Charlie and his family were up from Oklahoma City and spent the night. On Saturday, we feasted on snacks and desserts and sang Christmas carols together. The little ones sang solos of songs they learned, "Silent Night," "Oh Holy Night," "Here Comes Santa Claus," and "Jingle Bells."

Sunday morning, when we were all together, we opened our gifts. We served our Christmas dinner of ham and "all the fixin's" buffet style. After asking for the blessing, Bill sliced the ham. We gathered around our dining table, loading our plates with our choices, and sat wherever we wanted throughout our house. It was a good plan for our growing family.

Bill and I let our kids take charge and settled into comfortable chairs downstairs. We realized we had just had another fabulous and memorable family Christmas, hoping there would be many more.

Bill's Birthday Surprise.

It was a New Year, 2005. Without Bill knowing, I began planning a special birthday celebration for his 80th birthday on April 11. I would have a surprise open house for him on Sunday afternoon, the day before.

I designed the announcement-invitation notes and mailed them out to family and friends, both out of town and local. I was able to keep the secret from Bill until...

Bill began receiving birthday cards in the mail from some who could not attend the open house. He wanted to know what was going on. When I told him, he exclaimed, "Aw, your makin' too much fuss over my birthday." I saw his dimples deepen. He was smiling deep down inside.

Yard decorations for Bill's birthday.

On his open house day, guests started coming by one o'clock. There were former co-workers and long-time friends. His guests visited with him individually and in groups of families and friends. Our kids and grandkids visited with his guests and showed some of them through our home. Bill's birthday open house lasted into the evening and was hugely successful.

I had heard friends and family talk about having birthday celebrations to take in lots of gifts and money, and I knew Bill wouldn't want to do that. So, I had written on his announcements in bold letters: PLEASE RESPECT OUR REQUEST OF NO GIFTS. Because of this request, no gifts were sent or given to him for his birthday.

Charlie and Bill

Bonnie and Bill

Busy Times.

The summer and fall were like former years, but with grandkids of all ages, there was never a dull moment. The summer months were busy with guests much of the time.

Then again, we had grandkids spending extended time at our house while school was out.

With the coming of the fall months, most of our grandkids were back in school, so Bill and I had more quiet time to rest and relax by ourselves. We spent more time grocery shopping than usual, making plans for what we would prepare ahead of time for the holidays.

Bill, I, and our family celebrated Thanksgiving and Christmas as we had for years, including serving our dinners buffet style because there were now so many of us. The plan worked for us, and both holidays were memorable, exciting, and delicious. Now it was time to look forward to another year.

Our Spring Trip.

We both liked the greater peace and quiet the winter days brought. But Bill became restless and wanted to take another road trip in the spring. So was I. We arranged to go to Mountain View and made reservations at our favorite motel. We took a scenic, relaxing two-day drive on our way there.

Again, we checked back into our motel room. When we woke up from a good night's sleep, I dressed and hurried down to the breakfast buffet for the choice of foods we both liked. I chose our favorites of egg omeletes, biscuits and sausage gravy, and orange juise and hurried back to our room with them.

We took our time eating breakfast and drinking our decaf coffee. Just before noon, we walked the short distance to the festival grounds, where we found plenty of choices for lunch. Walking among the singing groups was pleasing and exciting; with each trip, we enjoyed them more than ever. The songs were what Bill and I heard in our childhood. A favorite was "Brighten the Corner Where You Are." This was the first hymn I heard in church in the schoolhouse.

After a few relaxing and fun days, we were ready to head home. Yes, Bill and I were eager to head back home again.

Bill and I would continue returning to Mountain View for as long as possible.

A Health Problem.

Bill had an appointment with his cardiologist soon after we got home. His doctor did a thorough examination. Then the nurse drew blood for Bill's lab tests. His doctor said he would let us know the results, often mailed to us.

The doctor's office called Bill to schedule an appointment with the doctor. We waited in his office, anxious and concerned about the test results. The doctor sat down and looked directly at Bill and told him the tests showed he had beginning kidney failure. And because of Bill's heart condition, he was not a candidate for dialysis.

Bill's health diagnoses and issues were stable with careful management of his medications. His doctor said blood transfusions might be needed and beneficial based on lab results and other tests. In a few weeks, the doctor called and said Bill needed a blood transfusion and had scheduled an appointment.

We went together for Bill's blood transfusion appointment, and I sat with him during the procedure in an outpatient setting. It took most of the afternoon, and his cardiologist came by a few times to check on him. When he dismissed Bill, I drove us home. It took Bill a couple of days to regain his strength.

Some Changes.

Bill wanted to live as normal a life as possible. He continued to mow our lawn with his walk-behind power mower, and I made it a point to be out in the yard when he did it.

One day I noticed he had turned off his mower and sat resting before he finished. Trying not to be too obvious, I walked over to him and told him I would like to try mowing, too. He smiled and showed me how to start his mower. Bill and I finished mowing together that day. The rest of the summer, we did it together.

Bill paid our monthly bills, and we still had our joint checking account. One day, he sat down at the dining room table with a handful of bills and his checkbook. He asked me if I would like to write the checks for the bills, and he would put them in their stamped envelope.

I wrote the check for the first bill he gave me and

handed it back to him. He took the check and held it out in front of him. In a soft voice, he said, "Your handwriting is beautiful! It's just too bad you can't read it."

We both smiled at his quip. He continued handing me the other bills for me to write their checks. We enjoyed this "ritual" for the rest of our lives together.

Is It Time?

By early fall, Bill was resting whenever he could. We sat in our matching lawn chairs on the deck outside our back door. And he wasn't going down the stairs to our family room, even though it was his favorite room where he had set up his mini kitchen.

While in my nursing practice, I noticed husbands and wives who had promised never to put each other in a nursing home. Sometimes one or the other had to break their promise. I told Bill not to hesitate to put me in a nursing home if necessary, and he assured me he also wanted me to do the same for him.

Bill became preoccupied and restless, moving from one place to another.

One day, I was working at the island counter in our kitchen, listening to music. Looking up, I saw Bill standing in the kitchen doorway, and he wasn't fancy steppin' or snapping his fingers to the music.

He looked at me and quietly said, "I've been thinkin'. Do you think it's time for me to go to a nursing home?"

Shocked and saddened, I exclaimed, "Oh, no! As long as I can, I will take care of you. No, it's not time for you to go to a nursing home!"

Making Bill Comfortable.

I was always aware of needed alterations or mending on our clothes. Bill had lost weight over the last few months, and his jeans were baggy, a thing he hated. He was used to me altering his clothes before he asked.

To alter Bill's jeans as I wanted, I removed the belt loop in the back, loosened, and cut the waistband over the back seam. I carefully ripped out the back seam, cut the fabric to the needed size, and sewed everything back in place. He was really pleased. So, I altered his many other pairs of jeans and pants.

Bill turned the thermostat up and was wearing sweaters over his western shirts. He kept his closet well organized and in order. I noticed a group of western and plaid flannel shirts he seldom wore. When I asked him why he wasn't wearing them, he told me they only had one pocket, and he needed two pockets in his shirts.

To solve that problem, I worked on each shirt. I cut a square of fabric from the front shirttail to make a second pocket. Then I sewed a nice piece of cloth back where I had cut out the piece. I also slimmed the shirt down.

Bill tried it on the first shirt and left it on. He approved.

He had eight nearly new flannel shirts our kids had given him, and I made a second pocket for each. He was now warm and comfortable at home with the warm flannel shirts and fitted jeans.

Prophetic Words.

Bill's brother Bud and his wife Norma lived close to Jefferson City in the country. For several years, they had spent their winters in Texas in a community of retirees. They stopped at our place in late October on their way to Texas and were with us for Halloween. Norma had lived in the country all her life and had never seen trick-or-treaters. I had stocked up on treats. As Norma eagerly handed them out to the kids, I estimated we had over a hundred trick-or-treaters.

After several days, Bud and Norma headed to Texas for the winter.

A couple of days later, Bill and I were eating our lunch on TV trays and watching TV. I sensed he wanted to say something he felt was important.

He turned the TV off and said quietly and hesitantly, "Ya know, I've been thinkin.' Sometimes when things happen, the weather is bad, and it's dangerous to travel. We had a good visit with Bud and Norma. If something happens, tell them not to try to come back." His words turned out to be prophetic.

The Motor Home.

Bill and I were seeing his cardiologist regularly for assessment. Lab results were usually within normal levels. Occasionally, there were adjustments in his medications. He seemed upbeat and talked about the year ahead. His attitude was contagious to me.

Ever since we were married, Bill liked to check the

news in the daily paper. But he soon turned to the want-ads. He bought our used cars, boats, campers, and appliances from the ads.

One lovely Sunday, we were having lunch after church. Bill told me about a small, used motor home he saw in the ads. He said it was a nice day for a drive, and he wanted to see the motor home, just out of curiosity. He said he might know someone who would like it.

I knew Bill invested the extra income we had after selling our house in the country. The investment would mature and could be cashed in without penalty on January 2nd, about $10,000. But what does that have to do with him now?

It was a beautiful late fall afternoon for a long drive. We arrived at the owner's house and saw the small motor home, and we looked inside and liked the arrangement. Bill started the motor and listened to it for a while. He felt there were no serious concerns. He checked the tires, and they were nearly new. He asked me what I thought.

It was happening so fast and unexpectedly. I always told Bill that the investment was his to do as he wanted.

He visited with the owner and told him he liked the camper but wouldn't have the money for several weeks. The owner said maybe they could make a deal.

He said no one had any money so soon before Christmas, and they wanted him to sell the motor home to them on payments. Bill asked me what I thought.

I said, "Go for it!" I was still processing the deal, but I thought, "If that's what you want, I'm okay with it."

Bill didn't tell me the price, but he knew I recalled it was less than $5,000. He told the young owner he wanted the motor home but would have the cash on January 2nd to buy it and take it home. The owner smiled, and he and Bill "sealed the deal" with a handshake. It was the month of November. I'll write later about how the deal turned out.

Ending the Year.

We were all concerned about Bill's health issues and determined to make the upcoming holidays as festive as ever, or more so if possible. He made several of his delicious pumpkin pies for Thanksgiving. As we all gathered, we loaded the dining room table with our traditional favorite foods. The desserts were on our dinette table in the living room downstairs. We all feasted as we enjoyed, yes, our best Thanksgiving ever.

With Christmas on the way, Bill said he would not go shopping at the mall. He said it was too much walking. I thought so, too. I had suspected that and had shopped from catalogs for a few weeks. Some of our grandkids liked, even preferred, our monetary gifts. They usually liked the size and color.

We gathered on the weekend before Christmas on Saturday night. My friend, Santa Claus, surprised us by coming through our front door and walking down the stairs with a hardy "hohoho," ringing his Christmas bells and laughing.

Sitting in our rocker close by, he gave the gifts I had left by our front door to the little grandkids and great-grandkids. Santa read "The Night Before Christmas" and waved goodbye as he ran up the stairs shouting, "Merry Christmas."

Sunday morning, we all gathered to exchange our Christmas gifts. The exchange took a couple of hours with the spouses of our grandkids and another great-grandchild. All of us gathering together was what made our Christmas so wonderful.

We set our dinner buffet style, with desserts on the family room's dinette table. But Bill decided not to make his fabulous pecan pies. He usually spent several hours rolling the crusts, making the fillings, and carefully arranging the half-pecan meats. No one said anything about the missing pecan pies. We were thankful that our Papa Bill was there with us.

After thanking God for our blessings of health and each other, we spent the afternoon dining on our ham and the fixins' and fabulous desserts. We visited and sang Christmas carols together, a cappella. Another fabulous family Christmas, maybe the best ever.

Bill and I sat together on our settee, spending our time "recovering" from our holiday celebrations. We were both thankful for our family and the many comforts of home. And we both appreciated each other and treasured the life we had together.

We were hoping, yes, praying for good health for the year ahead. We would surely need it for our... surprise to me... motor home. Bill could claim it on January 2.

Chapter Eleven
THAT'S LIFE

A Special Compliment.

Between Christmas and New Year's Day, Bill and I went on a road trip to Republic to visit my brothers, nieces, and nephews. More great holiday foods and treats.

On New Year's Day evening, we were content to sit together on our settee back home and watch TV. We were feeling well-fed, maybe overfed, and still snacking on leftover goodies from the Christmas holidays. It had been a wonderful family holiday season.

Over the past few years, I had become more health conscious. Maybe vanity also entered it because of being unable to get into some of my favorite clothes. I had lost a couple of dress sizes and still needed to lose a few more pounds, including those I gained during the holidays. I was determined to continue the progress.

As we were snacking, I told Bill, "I've got to get back to losing weight, especially those pounds I just gained."

Bill said nothing, and I wasn't sure he heard me. After a moment, though, he said, in a soft voice, "Nah, you're perfect just like you are."

I was speechless. Really, I was taken aback, but oh so pleased. No compliment could top that, even if it wasn't totally accurate.

Our New Motor Home.

Bill's health was fragile. When that happened before, they adjusted his treatments, and his health improved. But fragile health didn't stop him from living life to the fullest.

On January 2, he cashed in his investment and deposited the money, about $10,000, into our bank account.

Bill drove us the half-hour trip to get the '84 Toyota motor home he had bargained for with a handshake in November. He paid the young owner with a check, about $4,000. I drove our car, followed Bill as he drove his prize motor home, and parked it in our driveway close to the garage door. It got his full attention for the rest of the week.

The motor home was very small. Along one side was a narrow countertop and, in the back, a small table over the hide-a-bed. But there was no kitchen, and Bill set out to change that.

Even though the weather was cold and snowy. Bill and I went to the hardware store, bought a small refrigerator, a microwave, a hot pad, and a coffee pot, and set them up on the countertop. We brought extra dishes, silverware, and other useful items from our kitchen. And we grocery shopped and fully stocked the kitchen with favorite foods all on the day he bought the camper.

The next day, we had a tasty lunch in our motor home, which Bill kept heated all the time. We continued relaxing there in the afternoon but agreed not to spend our nights there.

We ate lunch in our "new to us" motor home all week. The weather continued to be cold and snowy. We listened to music and made plans for our spring trips.

An Old Country Girl Lives On

A Bad Sign.

Friday night of our relaxing, non-busy week, we were dressing for a, hopefully, good night's rest. Bill took his shirt off and asked me, "What is this?" He showed me a rash on his forearms.

What I saw shocked and devastated me. I knew from my nursing practice that the rash is known as petechiae. It is a tiny pinpoint, surface blood blisters on the skin, which is not a good sign.

"How long have you had these?" I exclaimed. "We need to get you to the emergency room."

"Why? What can they do, anyway?" Bill asked.

Understanding it was essential that the doctor know this, I put in a call to him.

Soon, Bill's doctor called back, and I described what was happening and that the petechiae outbreak was mild. He agreed to have Bill come into his office on Monday morning.

I let our kids know what was happening. It was a sad weekend for all of us. There was no rest that night for any of us and for many nights to come.

"I wanna go home."

By Saturday morning, we needed groceries. Bill chose not to go with me. As I was shopping, I bought him his $2.00 lottery ticket. When I gave it to him, he knew I had broken my rules of no gambling. The broad smile on his face was worth it all.

Monday morning, Bill's doctor saw him first thing.

After extensive lab tests, the doctor talked with us about the results. He said a series of blood transfusions might help his condition. The doctor strongly urged him to go to the hospital for admission to intensive care instead of going to the doctor's office every day for blood transfusions.

As soon as we arrived at the hospital, they admitted Bill to the Intensive Care Unit. They immediately started his IV and began his transfusion. After completion, they did more blood tests. His doctor came into Bill's room. He said there was some improvement, and they would give Bill another blood transfusion the next day.

Bill relaxed and dozed off, which was good since we had not been resting well. So, I hurried home to freshen up and headed back to him.

He was awake, and they brought supper trays for us both. They had "adjusted" the ICU rules for us, and they served me meals and allowed me to stay all night in his room, resting in an adjustable recliner close by him. I suspect it was his doctor's intervention.

Bill received blood transfusions the following two mornings, and they did more lab work. He was more than ready to go home. So was I.

After reviewing the lab work, his doctor came into Bill's room. We could tell by his expression that the report was not good. He had been Bill's heart doctor for over twenty years and became our good friend.

Bill was sitting up in bed, and I moved closer.

With Bill's chart in hand, his doctor told us that the transfusions weren't helping, and Bill's kidney function was decreasing. There was nothing more that could be done. He asked Bill what he wanted to do.

Without hesitation, Bill quietly but clearly said, "I wanna go home."

Bill's doctor wrote orders for him to go home the following day in an ambulance, with me by his side. He placed Bill on hospice and wrote orders for the hospice nurse to be at our home when we arrived.

The doctor shook our hands and turned away to the door. He had his hands over his face, and his back and shoulders were shaking with his quiet sobs as he left.

Slipped On Up to Heaven.

I called our kids with the devastating news and told them Bill would go home on January 11th. The day was also Connie's birthday (Charlie's wife), and they were away from home. They instantly changed their plans and drove to our house to be there when Bill came home. Also, Kathi, and Susan would be at our house when we arrived home.

John and his family lived near a small town close to Wichita. When I called to tell hm the new orders, he immediately said he would come to the hospital and spend the night with us. John is a quiet man, but his presence comforted Bill and me. The hospital set up a cot in the visitors' waiting room for John, but I doubt any of us slept very much.

Early the following day, John left the hospital and headed home for breakfast and a shower. He and his family would be at our house when his dad came home from the hospital.

Shortly after Bill and I ate breakfast, the nursing staff

completed Bill's paperwork. They called an ambulance to take us, at normal speed, to our home and carry Bill by a gurney to our bedroom. We propped him up in bed with pillows and his oxygen tubing. Kathi Suzi, Charlie, Connie, and I gathered around their dad's bed.

Bill was smiling, but quiet.

Bill was on hospice care. In my nursing practice, I cared for hospice patients, who often lived several weeks or even months, at least a few days. I couldn't allow myself to think of him not being with me.

He seemed to be comfortable. Bill was asking our kids about our grandkids and our great-grandkids.

As we were visiting, the hospice nurse stepped into the room. She asked me if I knew Bill's Social Security number, and I said I would have to look it up. Immediately, Bill spoke up and told the nurse his number.

Just a few minutes later, Bill took a few labored breaths.

I got on my knees on the bed beside him, holding his hand.

He looked at me with the soft blue eyes I loved so much. Then he closed them for the last time.

I knew his struggle was over. So much for a few more months, a few more weeks, or a few more days. Bill had quietly slipped on up to heaven.

It all happened so fast.

We told the hospice nurse what was happening. After examination and assessment, she declared Bill deceased. She called a hearse to take him to the funeral home. The nurse offered her condolences and quietly walked away.

Sadly, John drove up our driveway with his family when the hearse was leaving.

Honoring Our Loved One.

I could not think clearly. I thought I was prepared for this day; I was not. At the same time, our kids and grandkids were finding it difficult to deal with the passing of their dad and Papa. It helped that some of them stayed with me for a couple of days before returning home.

There were so many phone calls to make, both local and long-distance, and I wanted to be the one to tell everyone of Bill's passing. While making and receiving calls, I spent my waking hours on the phone for a few days.

It had been snowing for days throughout the Midwest, and several inches of snow were on the ground. It was the worst snowstorm ever recorded in the area. As a result, most of those living far away from Wichita could not come to Bill's memorial service.

I called his brother Bud and told him of Bill's passing. He said, "Norma and I will be there as soon as we can." They would drive into the storm.

I told him what Bill had said: "Sometimes when things happen, the weather is bad. If that happens, tell Bud not to come back." Bud knew the trip would not be safe, so he agreed to stay home.

I was on the phone constantly. There were several inches of snow on the ground. The snow and ice caused the power lines to break, and electricity was cut off in some areas. Gas pumps in Republic were closed. My family there could not come to Bill's memorial service.

My youngest brother, Walt, lived near Kansas City. Four-lane roads had not closed, but the snow was still falling. Walt and his wife, Gail, made the two-hundred-mile trip, anyway. He drove at twenty-five miles an hour to Wichita, and it took them over eight hours to get to our home. After visiting, they stayed with local relatives until Bill's memorial service.

Bill had told me he would like to have taps played at his funeral. He was a member of a veterans of war organization. So, I contacted the commander of the army base in Fort Riley, Kansas. He said he would send a small group of soldiers to play taps, give a twenty-one-gun solute and place a flag over Bill's coffin at the outdoor ceremony.

Even with the bad weather, there was a large crowd at Bill's memorial service. After the service, all our family and a few others followed the hearse to the cemetery for graveside services.

I had never considered not having graveside services for Bill. I learned later that the wind chill was twenty degrees below zero that day. His gravesite was on the cemetery's north side, and there was nothing to block the cold north wind as it blew across the fields.

We gathered around the coffin, draped in the American flag, for a brief graveside service and a prayer. The soldiers played taps and gave a twenty-one-gun salute. The salute comprised three riflemen, each shooting their rifles together seven times.

Two soldiers started folding the large flag over Bill's coffin. With the cold wind blowing so hard, their first attempt failed, and they had to unfold it and start over. We were shivering in the cold until the soldiers finally finished folding the flag and handing it to me. My heart hurt, but I managed to thank them, then we all hurried to our cars to get warm as we headed home.

The memories of that day will be with me forever.

Making Decisions.

I had never felt alone since Bill and I met when I was sixteen; it had been about sixty years. Now I had to go on without him. Our kids and grandkids, however, were ever-present with any help I needed. And Bill and I had our affairs in order, "Just in case something happened."

Many decisions needed to be made now that I was without Bill. Where would I go? Was I going to stay in the house? There were some offers for me to move in with family members. But I was too independent to give up my home.

Our house was much larger than I needed or wanted. After much checking, I decided to move to a gated senior retirement complex and lease a three-bedroom apartment by a lake. It was independent living, and I could have overnight guests for up to two weeks.

Getting ready to sell our house while it was still cold outside, I thoroughly scrubbed our three bathrooms and washed the many large windows on the inside. Then I had the carpets professionally cleaned, and they needed deep cleaning after our many get-togethers.

One day while I was cleaning, the front doorbell rang. When I opened the door, I found Jerry Self, our former realtor, standing there with a lovely flowering plant.

He smiled, handed me the flowers, and softly said, "Bill would want you to have these." He turned and quietly walked away.

It was February 14, and I shall always treasure the story.

Moving On.

Another change I needed to make involved the '84 Toyota motor home I didn't need. Bill had only gotten to enjoy it for a few days. Charlie bought it and took it to his home in Oklahoma City. He still has it.

Still moving forward, as soon as the weather allowed, I refinished our large back deck. Then I couldn't resist a rest in my comfortable reclining lawn chair. But Bill's empty matching recliner was sitting there close by, and it saddened me.

I moved on to my other tasks while preparing the house to sell. So, I weeded my flower beds where the flowering bulbs and other spring flowers were already making a beautiful display.

Before I sold our house, our granddaughter, Tracy, and her husband moved to Wichita from Oklahoma City to be near her Granny. Their former plans for work and a place to live didn't work out. So, they moved into our downstairs family room and made it an apartment. When the house sold, they moved to an apartment. Tracy and her family lived close by for several years.

The house sold for my asking price, and we closed the deal in July. I gave possession over the first of August. At the same time, I had signed a one-year lease with the gated apartment complex. Three bedrooms were what I needed for the heirloom antique furniture I still had. Eventually, I wanted to pass the prized furniture on to our family.

I had about two weeks to get moved, a short time to say goodbye to the last home Bill and I had shared. I had so many treasured memories that would stay with me forever.

My family helped me pack what we could. Then I hired a company to move me to the apartments. They unloaded the furniture and set it in place. I was so glad my family was there to help me get settled into my new home.

My apartment location was in a lovely setting. We entered through the back door, ground level. The sliding double-door opened onto a large balcony overlooking the lake on the other side of my apartment. I enjoyed the gorgeous sunrises.

Throughout late summer and early fall, I had several house guests. Some of those who couldn't make it to Bill's memorial service now came to visit and spend time with me. With guests and my family, I was never alone.

An Intriguing Trip.

In early September, I was invited to attend the wedding of one of my nieces, Kate, near Marion, North Carolina. She told me she and her fiance were going to be married, in the air, in the basket of a hot-air balloon. They could have a few guests, and they invited me to be one of them. I couldn't resist and said, "Yes!"

My only sister, Carol, Kat's mom, lived nearby. I flew there a few days before the wedding to spend time with her before the wedding. Then, on Saturday morning, October 20th, we gathered at the hot-air balloon airfield, and the balloon was there and ready to go.

The beautiful bride and the groom beckoned the few of us to board the balloon. Then they and the minister climbed into the basket. Quietly, the balloon began to rise, and we were airborne. The view was incredible as we rose higher.

Hot air balloon at wedding

The bride and groom exchanged their vows with the maid of honor and the best man standing with them. Then the minister said, "I now pronounce you man and wife. You may kiss the bride." And they kissed.

The balloon lowered slowly and landed softly, close to the waiting crowd. There was a huge wedding cake ready for the couple to cut and serve to the wedding guests and the large group of spectators. I visited with nieces and nephews.

And there was constant picture taking.

The next day, the newly married couple invited Carol and me to come to where they were staying for their honeymoon. They took us out to a nice dinner but didn't invite us to their suite. After all, it was their honeymoon. Instead, Carol drove us the few miles back to her apartment.

I flew back home the following day. The opportunity and experience of riding in a hot-air balloon had been too intriguing to pass up. Plus, being there for the wedding, of course. I'm glad I made the trip.

Our First Thanksgiving Without Bill.

Back home, I started planning for the holidays just ahead. I began cooking, especially for our family Thanksgiving get-together. This year would be difficult because it would be the first Thanksgiving without my beloved Bill... their dad and Papa.

When Thanksgiving came, we had a giant smoked turkey and all the trimmings. But Bill wasn't there this time to cut and serve it to us all.

Honoring him, I made Bill's pumpkin pies, which the family expected. They may not have been as good as his, but they were good. I didn't make his pecan pies. And our kids and grandkids brought covered dishes, salads, and desserts.

As I recall, all our family was there for this special family Thanksgiving time. In our prayers, we thanked God for the many years He gave us together.

I will forever miss Bill.

But I had a big project brewing for the near future to look forward to.

Chapter Twelve
TRIP TO CHINA

An Interesting Opportunity.

In mid-summer, after Bill's passing, I heard about a local congregation group planning a mission trip to a college in China in December. The group could go there as workers but not as missionaries, and our denomination had workers who were teaching there.

They wanted English-speaking people to come to their college classes, engage in conversation with their students, and socialize with them in the evening. And because it was the Christmas season, we could tell the students why we celebrated the holiday.

I had just sold my house and began moving to an apartment. I wanted to go to China but didn't know whether I could get my affairs in order in time to take the trip. I did.

Our denomination's mission board paid for the expenses for the two-week trip to the college. Each of us paid for the cost of the tour we later took to some landmarks across China. The money from Bill cashing in his savings account came in handy, leaving me with enough to pay for my share of the trip.

I was excited and intrigued to be going to China. I first heard about the country when I was five years old in my one-room country school. One day, the teacher brought a small world globe to school for us.

The older students in our school pointed out that we were on one side of the globe, representing earth, and China was on the opposite. They said the only way to get to China was to go straight through. But that was not true.

Arrival and Orientation.

The day after Thanksgiving, our nine women and man's group flew from the Wichita airport to the New York City airport. From there, we flew north and close to the North Pole. Flying south, we landed in the designated airport in China on Saturday afternoon.

With a tour guide, we loaded on a bus, taking us to the isolated city where the small university was. A few smiling teachers we would work with met us, and we went to one of their apartments and got acquainted with each other.

They gave us a thorough orientation about the students. They had grown up in the "back country" and lived in caves and tents. There were no houses, and the Chinese government had started schools through high school for them. Chinese teachers taught them basic English, and they needed English-speaking workers to help them improve their speaking.

China is known for its extensive railroad systems. There were railroads close to the student's homes, but they were a long distance from the college. We were told it took some students two or three days to get from home to the college. Some students went home in the summer, some didn't go home for four years, and some never again.

After the orientation meeting, they served us a fabulous buffet meal of authentic Chinese cuisine. We visited and got to know the college teachers. Most of the about three dozen teachers were workers from our denomination. Only a few of them attended our first meeting.

Our group was weary from the long trip and the time zone change. We each went with a teacher to share their apartment while we were there, and we were to show up with the teacher in the classroom the following day. But first, we needed a good night's sleep, and we got one.

Teaching the Meaning of Love.

On the first day, it was delightful, as were the rest. The students were eager and excited to speak English with us nonstop. The students engaged us in conversations between classes, asking us where we were from in the United States. Some of them knew the landmarks of our country. And the ability of some students to speak and understand English impressed me.

Whenever I asked students what they wanted to do after graduation, most of them said with a heavy accent, "I wanna go to America!" Whenever I encouraged the student to plan to go to America, I found it really was already their plan: "To go to America."

Teachers invited us to speak before their classes. One day I wore a lovely gold-colored T-shirt to the classroom. Printed on the front and back was a reference from 1 Corinthians 13, known as the Love Chapter, from our Bible. Prearranged with the teacher, I stood before a class of students and described how our Book explained "LOVE" as the best thing we can have in our lives. I told them that was why we were here with them.

Some students followed up with me after class, asking to know more about our Book. I told them the Book says we have anger, hatred, and wars without love. The T-shirt attracted a lot of attention, so I wore it on campus, almost like a "uniform." It encouraged conversations about our Book and how its teachings are our guide.

In the evening, the teachers invited a few students to their apartments, where each of our group was staying. Both the dorms and the teachers' apartments were on campus. Even though it was cold, and snow was on the ground, it was a short distance for the students to walk. They dressed warmly and were used to the cold weather.

Sharing About Christmas.

In planning for our trip, it was suggested that we bring Christmas decorations and holiday crafts. I took a large suitcase of craft materials for the students to make holiday decorations. We cut and pasted paper strips into colorful chains, hanging them around the room. We made twelve-inch stand-alone Christmas trees and lacy, paper doily angels.

The students asked about our Christmas holiday. We told them about our Book's story, how a baby was born many years ago. We told them how he grew up and taught us to love one another. Some students wanted to know more about the Christmas story, but they limited us to what we could tell them,. We could answer their questions and pray for them.

Members of our group were with students in the evenings. While making Christmas decorations, they made and baked cookies and snacked on them and other treats. The students were particularly fond of hot chocolate, so we always had it for them.

We enjoyed how polite and respectful the students were. And even though they were in college, they reminded me of young teenagers. They were so eager to talk with us and kept up a constant conversation, and that's just what we wanted.

My Special Coat.

Our group had free time to walk on sidewalks in the city close to the campus, but it was freezing. I was prepared. I made a warm, insulated trench coat many years before. The fabric was tapestry and had the "Children of the World" pattern woven into it.

There were one-inch faces and figures of children of all races, distinguishing their ethnicity and culture. Purses in the pattern were popular then, but there was no coat like mine.

One time while we were walking in the crowded city, a young woman walked up to me, smiling, and speaking Chinese. She pointed out the faces, reached out, and touched my coat sleeve. Even though I couldn't understand her, I felt she was clearly expressing how much she liked my coat.

Bonnie in special coat, entrance to the digs

A Shopping Experience.

We heard about a shopping center in the city within walking distance of the campus. One Sunday afternoon, our group went there. It was a huge five-story brick building. Venturing inside, we couldn't believe our eyes.

Each of the five stories had dozens of shops. There were escalators to move between levels, and no elevators were open to the public. We chose not to go to the fifth floor. We wandered around from shop to shop. Guess what? Most of the items were marked "Made in China."

The place was packed with shoppers, mostly foreigners like us. Some of our group made purchases, and I bought a few small toys for gifts for grandkids. All the while, the aroma from the food court taunted us. We each chose our favorite Chinese cuisine, sat down, and stuffed ourselves. Then we rewound our way back to campus.

We couldn't openly have a church service with students. Several of our group gathered to sing hymns and praise songs and join in prayer. It was one more wonderful, exciting day.

It had been a phenomenal two weeks with the students. The teachers had an open house so the students could go from one apartment to another, thanking us for our friendship.

The following day, we boarded the tour bus with the guide to begin our tour of the historical sites of China.

Terra Cotta Soldiers.

Our group was just a few of the tourists on the bus. We developed strong friendships among our members and stayed together for our tour. The forty or so others on the bus were also foreigners from many countries.

Snow blanketed the vast countryside. But with the sunshine, it was a beautiful couple of hours' drive to the first landmark on our tour: the Terra Cotta Soldiers' Museum. None of us had ever heard anything about terra cotta soldiers.

Our guide told us the story of a Chinese man in the 1930s. He was digging a well into the sandy soil. Several feet down, he struck something hard with his shovel. Continuing to dig around the object, he uncovered a terra cotta (clay) soldier, another, and another.

History and research show a rich emperor in the 1200s whose palace was several miles inland on a hillside. The emperor had his slaves mold and fire the clay soldiers. There were whole divisions of them in identical uniforms. Each face, though, was individually hand molded, and there were no two faces alike.

Over twenty feet of sand had washed down on the soldiers since the 1200s. Each soldier had to be individually and carefully uncovered, sometimes by hand, and moved to the museum for display in the arrangement they found them.

Uncovered digs

Bonnie Lacey Krenning

Terra cotta soldiers

There were whole divisions of foot soldiers and entire divisions of soldiers mounted on horses. Historians believe the emperor placed the clay soldiers in front of his palace to frighten and scare off his enemies.

The soldiers were large, over six feet tall. We know Chinese people as small people. Also, the horses were massive in body and build. Someone asked the guide if they exaggerated them in size to be more frightening to enemies, and he said no. He said there was a time in a part of the country where Chinese men were giants. And there was a breed of massive horses.

One thing stood out to me. The giant horses and buggies with a driver were sturdy, ornate, and magnificent. We were told they were for the generals and officers to go where they needed among the soldiers. They would be an essential part of a working army.

Terra cotta horses and buggy

When we were there, the restoration had recovered over six thousand soldiers, and they were still digging. I was there over fifteen years ago.

Some historians believe that when digging and restoration are complete, the Terra Cotta Soldiers will be the world's greatest manmade wonder of the world.

Visiting the Terra Cotta Soldier Museum was an amazing experience. We spent hours walking among the displays of clay soldiers and horses. And there were food courts of Chinese cuisine when we were hungry. Now our group was ready to move on to Beijing.

Beijing and Tiananmen Square.

We took the bus to an upscale hotel in Beijing, checked into our reserved room, freshened, and dressed up for dinner in the hotel restaurant that served Chinese cuisine. The servers kept plates and bowls of food constantly before us. A lovely evening.

The next morning, we left the hotel into the beauty of Beijing, a mass of ancient architecture and artwork. The emperor's palace, built in the 1400s, is now a museum. It is a massive structure with over eight thousand rooms for family and workers.

The beauty of the magnificent buildings and artwork was beyond anything we could have imagined. In addition, they showed us pictures and told of the hundreds of acres of beautiful flower gardens in Beijing. But snow covered them when we were there.

Our guide took us to the historic Tiananmen Square, recognized as the largest public square in the world. In 1989, students protested there. They brought in troops, and they killed many students. The protest is known as the '89 Democracy Movement.

Bonnie and group at Tiananmen Square

By late afternoon, we were pleasantly exhausted and more than ready to return to our hotel rooms. Our guide reserved a table in the restaurant for our small church group. They served us a five-course meal of Chinese cuisine, fabulous beyond belief. Most of us managed a taste of everything.

The Great Wall.

After a good night's sleep, eating breakfast in our hotel rooms, we boarded the bus for the next trip to the site I wanted to see more than any other: The Great Wall. I learned about it in my one-room country school.

We arrived near the entrance to the wall. The area was like a small city, with shops and food courts abounding. After eating lunch, we went by bus to the entrance of the Great Wall.

Our guide said they built the first wall in BC to protect and guard the emperor against his enemies. They rebuilt it in 221 AD and rebuilt again in the 1500s. The wall was over five thousand miles long, built along the natural ridges of the mountain tops. They have restored about five hundred miles to accommodate tourists within the past hundred years.

I always believed they built the wall to accommodate horses, buggies, or soldiers on horseback. Not so. There were steps to accommodate foot soldiers and guards, and they carved the steps from the natural rock.

Entrance to Great Wall

Some steps were six inches deep, and some were two feet deep. Some were six inches high, and some were two feet high. Short as I was, I had to climb onto the step by placing my knee on it and climb up on it. Standing in the center of a step, I could reach and touch the three-foot solid sides of the wall.

We were free to explore as we wanted. Our church group walked up the steep steps to a lookout tower about a mile away. When we reached the tower, we looked out over the vastness of China. I felt like I was "on the top of the world."

Other tourists walked further on. Our group chose to relax and continue to enjoy the view before carefully walking back down the uneven steps to the entrance to the wall.

It had been another fabulous day, and I felt like, "Now I've seen it all."

Ending a Phenomenal Experience.

We headed back to our hotel. In our rooms, we dressed for a formal evening at the hotel restaurant. We thoroughly enjoyed the meal of Chinese cuisine, knowing it would be our last one.

We were ready and happy to be going home soon. After breakfast in our rooms the following day, we dressed casually and boarded our tour bus to take us to the airport.

Our flight home was uneventful. We did, though, regain the twelve hours we lost going to China through time zones. We landed at a New York airport, and after changing planes, we flew back home to Wichita. The trip was a phenomenal experience, more than I could ever have dreamed. But "There's no place like home."

Remembering Bill.

It was just one week before our family get-together for Christmas. Our family had decorated our forever Christmas tree at our Thanksgiving get-together. And I had completed most of my shopping by mail. It helped that some of our grandkids liked monetary gifts.

As it got closer to our family get-together the weekend

before Christmas, the weather turned bad, with several inches of snow. Charlie and his family braved the almost impassable roads from Oklahoma City. Connie bravely drove part of the way, a traumatizing experience for her.

Santa Claus knew Bill had passed on. He was eager to be with us that year. Even though the roads were slick and dangerous, he "flew in" and brought a lot of joy to our Christmas. His reading of "The Night Before Christmas" and his hardy "Hohoho" were welcomed by all.

Having all our family together meant the most to all of us. Yes, we had gift exchanges, and our kids and grandkids brought most of the food, except the ham I served.

After our buffet dinner, we read the Christmas story of baby Jesus' birth and sang Christmas carols, as was our tradition. We reminisced about their dad's and Papa Bill's life, discussing the pleasant, fun times we had with him. We celebrated the best we could, sometimes tearfully.

Another year without Bill by my side. He and I both had what we wanted in our life together: "A home and a family."

I'll honor Bill in the days and years ahead.

Chapter Thirteen
LIFE IS WHAT YOU MAKE IT

Getting Settled.

To reach the lawn by the lake from my apartment was a process. I had to go downstairs into a hallway and out the door to ground level. I wanted my front door to open there instead, and I found a two-bedroom I liked that would be available on July 1st when I wanted it.

Over the past year, I passed some of my collectibles on to our family, and I could use a two-bedroom apartment at a greatly reduced cost. Another advantage was a laundry room next to my back door in the hallway. My apartment didn't have a washer and dryer.

I renewed my annual lease on July 1st. I still had massive pieces of furniture, so I hired movers to move them. My family helped me move the small stuff.

We could now walk out of my large, sliding glass double-door, onto the lawn, and down to the lake. Our family enjoyed many exciting days fishing, splashing on the water's edge, and riding in the paddle boats, a favorite pastime for them and me. And there were swimming pools throughout the complex where they could swim when they wanted.

Word of my new home on the lake spread around among family and friends. Frequent out-of-town guests came to spend a few days with me in the relaxing atmosphere. That summer, our kids, grandkids, and great-grandkids spent many happy hours with me, which I loved.

I Could Still Do It.

Even though I hadn't worked in nursing for a few years, I kept my Advanced Practice Registered Nurse (APRN) license renewed every two years in my birth month. The continuing education courses for my license were master's level. I did it "just in case" and "just to prove I could." I was in my late seventies.

A nursing home close by was advertising for a part-time position for an Assistant DON (ADON). I made an appointment with the Administrator and DON for an interview and brought a copy of my resume. Without looking at them, the administrator said, "You have the ADON position if you want it." I did. The pay was good.

After two weeks of orientation, I expected to go to part-time work. Not so…. The DON was planning to take a vacation, and she had not had a vacation for two years. Only after my orientation, she told me I would be in charge as DON for her week-long vacation.

It turned out, though, that she was a golfer and wanted to follow tournaments throughout the country. After a week, the administrator told me the DON would be gone another week, and then another, and then another. She took a month's vacation.

During my orientation, I noticed staffing shortages in nursing, both the CNAs and licensed staff. Working as DON, I would get calls early in the morning of an unexpected nursing absence, and I would go in and pass meds in their place. The meds had to be passed, and I worked a lot of overtime while the DON was on vacation.

When she returned from vacation, she assigned me to get the staffing stabilized and in place. From previous experience, I learned the best way to do that is to raise their wages to the highest reasonable level for each employee.

I was assigned to do the payroll for the nursing staff, something I had never done before. It is not usually a nursing task. It helped me, though, to identify the wages being paid and the need to make increases in pay for some staff. I made recommendations to the DON and administrator. As they made increases in adequate compensation, staffing retention improved.

But I wanted to work part time. To do what they expected of me, I had to work overtime. The pay was good, but I didn't need it. My family was more important, and I had proven to myself and others that "I could still do it." So, before the holidays, I turned in my two-week resignation.

Once again, I felt blessed to have my family close by me. In my nursing practice, I often noticed residents and patients who did not have anyone to love or anyone to love them. I was so thankful to be well enough to have my family in my home for the holidays. And they all chose to be there.

First Holidays Without Bill.

The weekend before Thanksgiving, we all gathered at my home. Some things were always the same; some things weren't. This year there was no Bill. With our growing family of grandkids and now great-grandkids, things were "a-changin'." Our precious kids and grandkids brought in a wonderful variety of covered dishes, casseroles, salads, and desserts, as they had done in the past. I continued the tradition by making the smoked turkey with rice dressing and pumpkin pies.

Bonnie's Rice Dressing
I made rice dressing for the first Thanksgivig Bill and I spent in our camper after we were married. I saw the recipe in a magazine. And I made this for as long as our family was gathering. It was expected.

The only difference was using rice instead of bread or cornbread. I added cooked, chopped chicken and more sweet peppers, celery, and onions than the other recipe called for.

We enjoyed our Thanksgiving buffet throughout the afternoon. At the same time, our kids brought my "forever" Christmas tree out of storage with all my Christmas decorations. The memory of getting it with Bill was a precious one. My family set the tree up for me and decorated it together.

Although it was a slightly sad time for me, I was in the mood to do my Christmas shopping. Catalog shopping was so easy. I phoned my order into the company, paid by credit card, and waited for it to arrive at my door. I did, though, shop in the local stores and found things I didn't know I had wanted. When the time came for our family get-together for Christmas, I was ready.

Christmas that year was on Saturday, so we gathered

a whole week before that. I had a full house of overnight family guests. Saturday evening, we snacked on the foods and treats everyone brought. I added bowls of fruits, which we all enjoyed.

Santa "surprised us" by showing up with a bag of toys for the little ones. As always, he read *The Night Before Christmas* and led us in singing *Jingle Bells*. With a hardy "Hohoho," Santa rushed out the door into the night to catch his sleigh.

Some of our families didn't see each other often. We spent the evening visiting and singing Christmas carols a cappella. Finally, it was time to get a good night's rest before our exciting day tomorrow. Having come up from Oklahoma City, Charlie, Connie, and family spent the night with me.

All our family managed to get together the following morning to open our gifts. We wanted to hand the presents out one at a time, little kids first. Because there were so many of us, our gift exchange took most of the morning, as we enjoyed seeing each other open their gift.

Again, as in the past, our kids and grandkids were pleased to bring favorite covered dishes, casseroles, salads, and a large variety of desserts. I prepared the ham and baked cinnamon rolls, as always. The cinnamon rolls were a favorite… and expected by all.

Bonnie's Favorite Salad
I had no recipe for my tossed salad which everyone seemed to like.

I started with a large bowl of colorful leaf lettuce.
Next, I added chopped celery, green onions, sweet peppers, and fresh tomatoes.

The finishing touch was for each person to add their preferred salad dressing.

No matter what we did, it was not the same without Bill, Dad, Papa.

Getting Concerned.

The few weeks before spring was a time to relax. Even in cold weather, though, I frequently had out-of-town guests, including my siblings, nieces, and nephews, and I welcomed them and enjoyed them.

As spring came closer and it warmed up, we walked out my front door onto the lawn and down by the lakeside. The water was still too cold to be in, but both kids and adults fished from the shore with some success. And some of us always took turns riding in the paddleboat, which held four people.

Our family often had potluck dinners and suppers, usually over twenty kids and grownups. The kids played games on the lawn outside my door, and I could see them running and hear them talking, laughing, and playing together, having a good time.

Then one warm summer day we were together, and the kids played on the lawn. My phone rang, and it was a call from the main office. They said they were getting complaints from other residents that our kids were making too much noise.

I talked with the kids, asking them to stop being so noisy. They quieted down for a while, but "kids will be kids."

Throughout the summer, when our kids were playing together, I would get a call from the office to quiet them. But the kids' playing and laughing was "music to my ears."

Concerns were adding up for me. I missed having my own washer and dryer, and I missed having a flower garden. And I liked living where I had families for neighbors next door. I realized that moving to this apartment complex may not have been the right or best decision for me. I did, though, renew my lease for another year.

Another Change.

Summer had passed. The kids were back in school, and I could relax and enjoy the quiet time. I could have, but I didn't. Instead, I looked for apartments where families of all ages, and singles, young and older, lived as neighbors. I found one and two-bedroom apartments, upper and lower level with stairways, and every apartment had a washer and dryer. And I could have flowers.

Our family celebrated Thanksgiving and Christmas in our usual yet unusual custom and manner. We visited together and always sang together in a Capella harmony. We feasted on our family's fabulous foods, along with my usual additions. Again, missing Bill, Dad, and Papa was the hard part for all of us.

During the former winter in my apartment, I ran up a huge heating bill each month. It was happening again. My master bedroom had a large, uninsulated plate-glass window overlooking the lake. When I talked with the management, they said there was nothing they could about the window.

Even with an electric blanket, my bedroom was often too cold for me to sleep there, and I slept in my spare bedroom. The only shower was in my main bedroom, and I bought a small electric heater to keep my shower warm enough.

I knew I didn't want to spend the rest of my life in this apartment complex. During our holiday get-togethers, I discussed with our kids about making the change. They encouraged me to do what I wanted. But my lease wouldn't be up until July 1st.

I wanted to make the right decision, so I looked at several apartments. The one I described before seemed to me to be the best choice. So, I revisited it. They had a one-bedroom apartment that would be available on June 1st, but it was now occupied.

They showed me a demo, but I did not know which apartment I would have out of over a hundred ground-level ones. It would be a one-bedroom, yes, a one-bedroom. I signed a lease contract which would become effective on June 1st.

What was I going to do with my many pieces of antique furniture? John offered to rent storage space for the large pieces, which solved my problem.

I arranged with a moving company to come to my old apartment and take my furniture to my new home. John moved what I didn't need to storage.

The apartment had a wood-burning fireplace on the north wall, so I placed the fireplace Bill and I made in my bedroom. I gave my antique bedroom set to Susan because there was no room for it in my bedroom.

Before winter came, I had an insert of a "pretend"

log set in the firebox of the living room fireplace. It had a realistic-looking flame with adjustable heat or not, as I chose. A good plan because I didn't want to deal with carrying wood or with messy ashes.

Enjoying My New Home.

One important task the day I moved was to set up my bed for the night. It was the wrought iron bed in which Bill was born. It was hot outside, but I turned on the "pretend flame" in the fireplace Bill and I made. Pleasantly exhausted, I soon fell asleep in my new home.

After moving, I needed to vacuum my former apartment, which I did. I turned in my keys on June 30th. I was confident that I had made the right decision this time.

Within a few days of moving, I started digging flower beds and setting out blooming plants I purchased from local nurseries. The fenced swimming pool was across the sidewalk in front of my apartment. As kids and grownups walked by on their way to the pool, they stopped and talked with me, welcoming me to the neighborhood. Sometimes I picked a small flower and gave it to a child.

For several weeks, I worked on getting settled into my new home. Throughout the summer, our grandkids visited and swam in the pool. We didn't have a lifeguard, so I went with them, not swimming, just relaxing in the shade and visiting with neighbors. My apartment was in an ideal location, rather than a location several buildings away from the pool.

Back to Part-Time Work.

Nursing was again beckoning me. A former co-worker knew about my success with wound care in the past, and she told me about a DON in a nursing home close by who was advertising for a part-time wound care nurse.

I was not a certified wound care nurse. Still, Continuing Education classes and my prior practice had prepared me for successful outcomes with wound care. I called and made an appointment to be interviewed for the part-time position.

I sat down with her and the administrator for the interview. As we sat together in the DON's office, she said, "We are familiar with your credentials and your success with wound care in your nursing practice." Smiling, she said, "You are hired if you want the position."

The DON described what the position entailed. They admitted rehab patients to the facility to be treated for pressure wounds, slow-healing surgical wounds, and any other slow-healing skin problems.

The wound nurse position was part time, and I could name the time when I wanted to work. No need to work weekends. *How hard could that be?* And the hourly pay was the best. I took the wound nurse position and had a few days of orientation before I took charge.

One of My Worst Cases.

I soon experienced one of the worst cases I had ever seen. The elderly woman was large, obese. Her husband was at the wheel as she tried to get into the car. She slipped and fell with her leg under the car, and the tire rolled against her leg and pealed a patch of skin loose on her right thigh. She was treated in the emergency room and sent home with orders for follow-up care.

Soon the site became infected, and they admitted her to the hospital for treatment. With IV antibiotics and careful cleansing, she became free of infection. They transferred the woman to our facility rehab for follow-up care until she could have a skin graft.

But where would they get a good patch of skin that large? The missing skin area was an irregular six-inch size. After my orientation, I took charge of her wound and requested that no one else do her treatment, and the DON honored my request.

I had never treated such a large wound. After evaluating the condition of the injury, I consulted with the woman's doctor. She agreed to order the meds and treatments I believed would work best for the patient.

When I began my nursing practice, the common practice was to let a wound "scab over." The current course was to cleanse the site of all infections and place a sterile, transparent dressing over the wound, preventing it from scabbing over.

After several days, the wound showed signs of healing. Removing the transparent dressing, I could plainly see

how the skin edges were gradually closing in and covering the wound site. After a few weeks of treatment, the new skin had grown over the wound site, with only a small area about the size of a lemon.

The resident was now walking again. Her doctor

dismissed her to her home with a follow-up of home licensed nursing care. I worked with her doctor to ensure they gave her the best in-home care. Later, I heard the wound had healed entirely, and no skin graft was needed.

Ending My Career.

After a few weeks, they asked me to oversee all the wound care in the facility. With input from the nursing staff, the doctors and I worked together, writing, and rewriting orders for the most successful current treatments for wound care. As an APRN, I could write orders, but the doctor had to sign off on them.

Since I had the flexibility to work when I wanted, I spent time on both day and evening shifts. I worked with the nurses, evaluating their work, and demonstrating the importance of treating in a way that aided healing. There was an improvement in wound care, and patients were discharged sooner.

Word got around about our success with wound care, and we became known as a wound care rehab. There was a gradual, or not so gradual, increase in-patient admissions for wound care.

After a few months there, I decided I didn't want to work in nursing anymore and wanted to retire. I was seventy-nine years old and wanted to spend more time with my growing family.

I turned in my two-week resignation.

But it wasn't over. The DON asked me to spend two weeks working with the nursing staff to establish a written plan for wound care. I held an in-service meeting with the nurses to better assure compliance to the plan.

It was a new freedom to know I would no longer be practicing nursing. Even though I started late in life, I had practiced nursing for over thirty years. However, I kept my

APRN License current until my ninetieth birthday month. It had been quite a trip.

My Huge Undertaking.

While working part time, I continued making my apartment my home. I wanted to hang family pictures and framed mementos on my walls. But the wall color was a drab off-white, and I wanted a warm color to brighten up the rooms. The apartment manager gave me permission to paint it the color I wanted if I bought the paint.

I chose a warm, blush color for the walls and white for the ceiling. With my stepladder in hand, I painted the ceiling first. When I started painting the walls, I soon realized I had taken on a huge task. So, I painted for three or four hours a day, two or three days a week. It took a couple of months to complete the painting, but I did it. Our kids and grandkids wanted to help, but I wouldn't allow them to do it.

Throughout the summer and fall, I had families over for pizza or Mexican food. They often insisted on bringing the food. I didn't prepare whole meals but attempted to make Bill's beef stew with some success. And I usually made the favorite pies, cookies, and other goodies they liked… and expected.

More Holiday Changes.

Our family get-together for the holidays was taking on a new look. I only had room for a few guests at a time in my apartment. Our kids and grandkids now had their own family gatherings, and they invited me to them. That worked out well for Thanksgiving.

Making plans for our gathering the Saturday before Christmas was a challenge. I reserved a separate area in a local buffet restaurant for our family, promising at least twenty guests. As they came in, I arranged for our family to give my name and they admitted them to our area. I took care of the bill.

The plan worked out well. We could fill our plates with the foods and goodies we liked and wanted. And my friend Santa showed up. He didn't bring gifts this time, but he visited with the little kids, asking them if they had been good and what they wanted for Christmas.

As always, Santa read *The Night Before Christmas* and led us in singing *Jingle Bells*. We noticed other customers joining in and singing with us. As he was leaving, Santa visited with other children in the restaurant.

The restaurant get-together was a good choice and a success. We lingered for over two hours, visiting and eating from the buffet as we chose. Before we left, I gave each one a Christmas card with a monetary gift.

Our Christmas celebration was not over. As with Thanksgiving, our kids and grandkids now had Christmas dinners in their homes. They invited me to all. It was an excellent way to celebrate our Christmas. No one mentioned it, but we were all missing Bill. And always will.

I had a quiet few days after Christmas, before New Year's Day. Plans were brewing, though, for an exciting year ahead.

Chapter Fourteen
WHO I AM AND MORE

A New Interest.

It was the beginning of many eventful years ahead.

I attended my church close by, where Bill and I belonged and attended when we weren't traveling. There were old friends from past decades who were always welcoming, and over time I made many new friends, both young and old. I resisted the "opportunities" to sing in the choir and teach Bible classes.

It was exciting to watch the spring perennial bulbs and flowers I planted the previous year opening and blooming. My flowers were a delightful attraction for my apartment neighbors as they walked by on their way to the front office, mail room, and swimming pool.

I now had several grown-up grandkids who were driving and lived close by. I usually had them over around their birthday. When that didn't work out, I mailed each one a birthday card with their "present" tucked inside. Everyone received a birthday card with the same amount, including in-laws and significant others. In addition, I often gave the little ones a small toy.

I was starting to do genealogy research to find who my mom's birth father was. Mom knew she was born when her mother (Maggie Barnard) was seventeen and unmarried.

Maggie, though, was "promised" to William (Billie) Stroer.

For several years, I had been asking those who I thought might have some knowledge of the circumstances. Mom was born close to where Clara, my oldest brother's wife, grew up. Clara's father was a brother to Billie Stroer, Mom's stepfather. Clara's folks belonged to the little country church where they and the Barnards, Maggie's parents, also belonged.

One day Clara and I were visiting and talking about old times. When I told her I would try to find out who Mom's birth father was, she told me this story.

Starting My Project.

Clara said her mother told her that my mom's birth father and his family were members of the same country church. "The man's name was 'Kenney,' and he had a funny first name." Those dozen words, spoken in five seconds, became the foundation for my research.

This all happened in Cedar County, Missouri, near Stockton. It was over two hundred miles from my home in Wichita. And Stockton was about twenty miles from El Dorado Springs. I was familiar with Stockton because Bill and I often drove there while attending the El Dorado Springs Picnic for a few days.

With spring on the way, I made plans, drove to Stockton, and stayed in a motel. With help from the courthouse staff, I searched the courthouse's census, birth, and death records. The old ten-year census records were handwritten, faded, and challenging to read.

I soon realized I would need some help. After a couple

of trips to Stockton, I found it. The Cedar County Historical Society (CCHS) office was just across the street from the courthouse.

I became acquainted with some members and joined the society. One member asked about working with me to find who Mom's birth father was. I told her about the name "Kenney," and the "funny" first name, and the country church they attended.

Danial Mitchell "Mitch" Kenney

Exciting Information.

I enjoyed driving the trips, but always missed Bill being with me. When I arrived in Stockton on one of my trips, the CCHS researcher was excited to have information that may prove helpful to me. In our work together, we had become friends. I took her to lunch. After the meal, she described what she had found for me.

According to the records, the David Barnard family, and the Danial Mitchell (Mitch) Kenney family lived on adjoining farms in Cedar County. Their families attended the same country church.

In the late 1870s, tragedy struck the Kenney family, and Mitch's wife died in childbirth. Fortunately, the baby lived. Mitch was in his late thirties and had children of all ages.

We can only speculate about how it happened, but a few months after Mitch's wife died, Maggie became pregnant at sixteen. It had been whispered that Mitch offered to marry her, but David, her father, wouldn't allow it.

There was no documented proof of who the birth father was, and Mom's birth was not reported in the records. A few weeks after Mom was born, when Maggie was seventeen, she married Billie Stroer.

First Success.

Now it was up to me to discover who Mom's birth father was. My CCHS friend searched for Kenneys in the area and found quite a few. One man was a descendent of another of Mitch's children. His name is Larry Kenney.

He owned an auto repair shop in Everton, a small town southwest of Stockton. When I called Larry on the phone, he seemed surprised… but not too surprised. When I told him my story and described the possible link between us through Mitch, Larry said, "He was a rounder."

Larry agreed to do DNA testing with me, and I ordered DNA test kits for us. We decided on a date for me to go to his shop to do the testing, and I went there on a Saturday afternoon. After doing the tests, Larry and I visited for a couple of hours about the Kenney family before I headed home and mailed the tests for evaluation. It took about three weeks to get the results back in the mail.

The result showed a sure match. It was good to finally know "Who I Am."

Capture and Escape.

I went to Stockton for a few days every three or four weeks. I mainly checked the census records to verify, if possible, some stories handed down by David Barnard and his family.

David and Rhoda Bernard

David told his family that he was born in a rural farm settlement in West Virginia. There were tribes of Indians living in the woods close by. One day, when he was sixteen, he and his older brother hunted in the woods.

While David and his brother were hunting, the Indians captured both. He said they arrived at the Indian encampment and were required to fight a duel with an Indian opponent. David said that his brother lost and put to death. David said he won his duel, and his life was spared, but he remained a captive.

David planned to escape as soon as possible. He claimed that the things he learned while living with the Indians enabled him to do so two years later.

One day he slipped away into the woods alone, and he knew the Indians would soon come searching for him.

He found a large hollow log, laid down and backed inside of it, and pulled leaves inside to cover the entrance. He was sure if they saw him, it would mean certain death. David said he heard the Indians talking and walking over the log where he was hiding. They did not discover him. Then the Indians walked away.

When David was sure they had moved on, he crawled out of the hollow log and started running in one direction into the night. After several hours, he reached a riverbank where a passenger boat was anchored. According to David, he told his story to the boat's captain and convinced the captain to let him ride to the next town.

David said the trip to the next town took several days. He became acquainted with a young woman who worked on the boat. Her name was Rhoda Grant, a niece of President Grant. She was working on the boat to pay off a debt owed by her father, a brother of the president. She and David developed a friendship that soon became more: marriage.

The Truth.

Not so. The story about being captured by the Indians is complete fiction. His marriage to President Grant's niece is also complete fiction. Records show his brother lived to old age.

Truth is, David was born in West Virginia and grew up there. One of his childhood friends was Rhoda Grant, but she was not President Grant's niece. At the time, Grant was a common name, as was Rhoda. President Grant's niece lived hundreds of miles from where David lived, and their paths never crossed.

Whew!

The truth is the birth records show David was born in 1840 and his wife, Rhoda, was born in 1841. Marriage records show the couple was married in their late teenage years. He worked for local farmers to support their growing family. They had several children before eventually moving to Kentucky.

More Storytelling.

In the early 1880s, David applied for a land grant in northern Kansas, near Wilson, and moved his family there. After a severe windy winter, he decided to move to Cedar County, Missouri. I don't know why he chose Cedar County, and there are no records of relatives living there.

Rhoda passed on in 1906. David was retired and lived with his grown children, who welcomed him. We were told another story when we were growing up. Made possible only by David's descendants, who may have inherited his creative storytelling abilities after he passed away.

They told of how David was still riding horses at one-hundred-two years of age. The story was he went hunting one morning, riding horseback. After getting his desired "kill," he brought it home, and the women prepared their lunch. He ate lunch, laid down, and closed his eyes for a nap. He went to sleep and never woke up.

Again, not so. I learned that the story of David's last days was total fiction because of the research records that my friend from CCHS and I found. We looked through the census records recorded every ten years. The census taker went to each home and recorded, by hand, the information given orally.

In David's first census in Cedar County, he added a few years to his age in his records. David added a few years to his previously declared age in each ten-year census record over several decades. By the year he passed away, they documented his age as one-hundred-two years old. David's actual age was eighty-two years old.

His birth records in West Virginia show he was born in 1840. If David had been born in 1820, as he claimed, his father's well-documented birth records show he was born in 1818. His father would have been two years old when David was born. Truth is....

Our son, John, found records that showed David spent the last two years of his life in Kansas City, living with his daughter. He was in failing health and unable to live alone, and he was in and out of the hospital and died in Kansas City. He was brought back and buried in Wagner Cemetery in Cedar Springs. Even though he was eighty-two, his tombstone reads one-hundred-two.

More Stockton Trips.

While visiting Stockton, I became acquainted with Barnard descendants who lived in the community. I told them what the records showed, but they remained convinced that our Rhoda Grant Barnard was President Grant's niece. When they were growing up, their parents told them to behave themselves because they were related to a president: President Grant.

On another July trip, John, his son, Mark, and I drove to the Eldorado Springs Picnic. We listened to the music from the grandstand and wandered around by the booths and rides. We went on to Stockton to our reserved motel room.

When evening came, we went to a well-known local restaurant specializing in local cuisine. A specialty was catfish from the local lake. Add to that blackberry pie. They seasoned the foods with local herbs and spices. It was a delicious meal before bedtime.

John was into serious genealogical research. He wanted to explore the cemeteries in the area where many of my ancestors were buried. We spent a couple of days touring the cemeteries he had chosen before heading back home. It had been a pleasant trip.

A Special Find.

I had always wanted to return to our old homeplace where I spent my childhood years. It was about nine miles south of El Dorado Springs. I learned that the present owners had turned the farm into a private deer lodge. When we lived on the farm, there were no deer in the area. The owners had torn down our old, dilapidated house and built a modern deer lodge.

I found who the present owners were and called them on the phone. The man was excited to hear from former owners to learn the history of the place. He offered to meet me there and learn about the farm's history.

I drove there and pulled onto the side road, about a quarter of a mile from the deer lodge. When I got out of my car, the grass and weeds were knee and hip-high on me. I walked down the dirt road to the lodge, where the owner was waiting for me.

As we visited, he was interested and pleased to know how Daddy and my brothers had cleared the native land and built the house and barn from the native lumber they sawed on the farm. After visiting for a while, the owner asked me if anyone had ever been buried there, and I assured him, "Not while my family lived there."

The man said. "I have something to show you." He brought out a small handmade concrete tombstone they had found under the old house when they tore it down. The handwritten words in the concrete read: EARL FRANKLIN LACEY.

It was the tombstone Daddy made when Lil' Earl died and was buried in the cemetery nearby to mark his grave. We could not afford to buy a new one then, but a few years later, Daddy could buy a new one. He had then placed the one he made under our house, and I did not know he had done that.

The man thought I might want the tombstone and offered to carry it to my car. It had been an interesting and exciting day, except for the tall grass. But wait, there is more to the story....

An Itchy Problem.

I returned to my motel room, where I had a few snacks for supper. Feeling itchy and irritated after walking through the tall grass, I took a soothing shower. I saw tiny deer ticks attached and crawling on my skin, especially where my clothes fit closely.

The ticks were tiny and flesh-colored until the attached ones started filling up with blood. I picked or scratched off the ones I could see and took a long shower. I covered the itchy red spots with the antibiotic ointment I had and hurried off to bed. It was a restless night.

The next morning, I was still itching. When I looked, several visible ticks were filling with blood. Again, I scratched off all the ticks I could see and applied ointment. I now had large areas of skin covered with ointment.

I was ready to head home, so I dressed, packed my bags, and grabbed breakfast as I left.

Although it was good to be home, I was still in torment—yes, torment—from the itching ticks and inflamed and swollen sites. It had become my night-time routine to check for ticks, shower, apply ointment at bedtime, and settle in for a restless night. The next morning, I followed the same established routine.

Having heard of Lime Disease, I had never seen a case of it in my nursing practice, and I knew nothing of the signs and symptoms. I decided to research the symptoms and treatment for it. I quickly found that it is severe and life-threatening in older adults, and the mortality rate was high among them.

Research shows that the immune system in older adults is usually seriously low, impacting their ability to fight the disease. And there is no certain and accurate test to diagnose it. The tests can show negative when the person is positive for Lime Disease.

Eight days after I was home, I made a discovery. One morning while dressing, I looked in the mirror, and a deer tick had newly attached itself to my upper right chest just above my breast. And I quickly scratched it off.

Ticks had got into the luggage in my trunk, where I parked in the tall grass and weeds in the driveway to our former farm. I immediately washed and dried my clothes, hoping to rid myself of ticks. But there is, however, much more to my story....

Lime Disease.

The ticks were gone, but the red, inflamed patches remained on my skin. I developed aches and pains and a low-grade fever that wouldn't go away. Research showed that an elevated temperature was a symptom of Lime Disease. Finally, I went to my doctor.

When I told her what had happened to me, she was reluctant to treat me for Lime Disease. The doctor refused to give me the specific, high-dose prescription for it and dismissed me with a low-dose antibiotic prescription.

Because of my symptoms and the research I had done, I was convinced I had Lime Disease. I went home and called the clinic and asked to talk with management. When the receptionist answered the phone, I told her about my nursing background and the research I had done. She said, "Let me put you on hold."

A couple of minutes later, she told me to come back, and my doctor would give me the needed, specific, high-dose prescription for Lime Disease. My unsmiling doctor met me at the front desk and handed me the script I wanted and needed for treatment.

The dosage was a pill to be taken three times a day for twenty-one days. The pain and fever gradually went away, but I felt debilitated and weak. After treatment, it took a couple of weeks for me to regain my strength. Apparently, I had Lime Disease.

Since my research showed that Lime Disease in older adults is often fatal, I quickly worked on improving my immune system. I ate natural foods, took supplements, and exercised more. I recovered and felt well, until....

Changing My Ways.

About a year later, the Lime Disease came back. I had changed to a different health care provider, a nurse practitioner, by then. When I told her the symptoms, she immediately ordered the specific, high-dose treatment I had taken the first time.

The three-week intense treatment was hard for me to tolerate, but it again put the Lime Disease in remission. I hated the treatment and aftereffects but was glad I was still a survivor. I accepted the possibility of having to continue the treatments for the rest of my life.

I continued eating natural foods and cutting out

processed foods and soft drinks. It was a delightful experience. I felt I had always eaten well, but this was better. At the same time, I was improving my immune system. Guess what....

After three episodes of Lime Disease, one each year, the disease has never, ever, come back for over six years. I have had no symptoms and am still here, doing well. Improving my immune system has improved my overall health. And the natural foods are delicious.

Finished with Genealogical Research.

My trips to Cedar County to do genealogical research and see the old home place only took a small amount of my time. Back home, I kept busy with our family, who visited often and invited me to their homes. I enjoyed attending church and socializing with my friends.

I worked with my flowers from the last frost in the spring until the first frost in the fall, a pleasant, time-consuming task. I had spaded up over three hundred square feet for flowerbeds and bordered them with brick. Flowers were blooming throughout the spring, summer, and fall.

My apartment faced east, and I saw some colorful leafed plants which required full shade. On the north side of my apartment, I spaded up another thirty square feet of flowerbeds, bordered it with brick, and planted the colorful plants I liked and wanted.

After three or four years, I finished my research in Cedar County. There was now more time to relax, catch up on reading and watch TV, to keep up on current events. For the first time since my retirement from nursing, I had no big projects, until....

Volunteering.

Someone told me about a program designed for youth who were orphans and had aged out of foster care at eighteen years. They cut funding for foster care providers, and the youth no longer had a home to go to. They were literally on the streets.

The Wichita Children's Home had developed a state-funded program for case managers, teachers, and social workers to assist the youth in securing food, clothing, and shelter. They met with the youth at a designated location several days a week. Some needed their GEDs (General Education Diploma), and the workers assisted the youth in preparing, taking, and passing the test to get their GED.

The center was looking for volunteers to assist in food preparation for the youth. I took the "opportunity" to check out the program. Volunteers were required to take part in an orientation program to ensure we passed a background check to assure the youths' safety. After taking the afternoon session, they certified me to work there.

At the center, there were a few days of orientation for me. The building was in midtown, with a food pantry and large used clothing room. The youth center had a kitchen with a refrigerator and freezer, where we served lunch and much more.

Some youths were hungry when they came in the morning. We kept cartons of milk, dry cereals, juices, and coffee for those who wanted it. We also received some casseroles, soups, desserts, and limited monetary donations.

Volunteering two days a week, I planned the meals

for those days. To ensure having enough food for the youth, I started cooking lasagna, casseroles, beans, cornbread, and Bill's beef stew at home.

Best of all, I became acquainted with many of the youth. They often told me that my cooking tasted like their grandma's cooking. Most of them asked me if they could call me "Grandma." I was pleased to have them do that. I became known as Miss Bonnie and Grandma.

As I learned more about the food pantry and used clothing room there, I also began volunteering there. We had some nice used clothes, and I assisted the youth in choosing casual and dress clothes for their job interviews. They usually found shoes they could use.

A businessman once brought five big black plastic bags of clothes and shoes. There were the best quality dress and casual used clothes, and several nice pairs of shoes in the sizes our youth needed. The man said he was looking for the right place to donate the clothing and felt he had found it.

The food pantry at our center was for low-income people who qualified for the program and was a separate program from the youth center. I soon became acquainted with the volunteers there. Organizations in town provided food donations. But there was a need for volunteers to pick up the foods and bring them to our pantry.

When I told my niece, Linda, and her husband, Larry, about what I was doing and our need for help, they began picking up loads of food we had ordered from the Kansas Food Bank two days a week. They brought the food to our pantry and worked on unloading it for us.

Because I was cooking at home for the youth, I ended up working over twenty hours a week at home, in the clothing room, the food pantry, and the youth center. The youth were so appreciative. It was an exciting and rewarding time for me.

Need I say, I had taken the "opportunity" to volunteer to the max… maybe too far. It was difficult to leave the center. The meal program was going well and would continue after I left.

Volunteering at the youth center was one of the most rewarding experiences I ever became involved in. These youth didn't have a family who wanted them, and no one wanted to adopt them as their own. I became intensely aware of the blessings of growing up in a family that loved and cared for me.

Life After Volunteering.

After leaving the youth program, I spent the next few years caring for my flowers and sharing them with others, especially the kids in my neighborhood. And being a neighbor, a mom, a grandmother, a great-grandmother, and a great-great-grandmother, with more on the way.

Even though retired from nursing practice, I renewed my nursing license every two years until I was ninety years old, just to prove to myself and others that I could do it. After that, I no longer needed to prove anything. I still had my body of nursing knowledge and could research as I wanted.

As the holidays approached, our growing family had our usual, yet unusual, get-togethers. We gathered at the buffet restaurant a couple of more times, with Santa as our guest. But it had become difficult, in fact, impossible to get all the family together at one time. Each family began having its own Christmas celebration.

I was invited and attended each one. Tracy, our granddaughter, and Susan each had festive holiday get-togethers. They invited all who could be there, and I enjoyed both.

And I was doing many things to stay well, including my delicious, healthful way of eating. Going to the Y (YMCA) to exercise and walking outside when the weather allowed kept me in good shape.

This past March I turned ninety-one. I want to be as well as possible for as long as possible. I'm gladly working at it full time and enjoying every minute.

Chapter Fifteen
A LIFE FULLY LIVED

Early Significant Times.

As I think back over my early life, I recall the most significant times which made me who I am. There are three happenings in my early teenage years that forever molded my life.

When I was fourteen, I went to church regularly. I was trying to please God and everyone, so I could be good enough to go to heaven. I realized, as hard as I tried, I was failing.

Then one evening at church, when I was fifteen and a half, our pastor read from the Bible, "Come unto me, all ye who labor and are heavy laden and I will give you rest… and you will find rest for your soul." (Matt 11: 28-29 KJV). I responded to Jesus' invitation and surrendered my life to His keeping. At the 'invitation," I went forward and declared it publicly.

When they baptized me by emersion, the church choir sang, "Ring the bells of heaven, there is joy today, for a soul departed from the foe." It seemed I could hear those bells ringing. My decision was the foundation for the rest of my life.

I turned sixteen on Match 2 the following spring. On March 15, Bill and I met. He joked later that he picked me up off the street. That's not the full story. Bill was my first date… and my last date.

Bill and Bonnie wedding

Bill helped to make all my childhood dreams come true. We were married when I was eighteen and we were married for fifty-eight years. Our love for each other carried us through the hard times and the good times.

He passed on ahead of me, but Bill and I will be together forever in heaven someday.

My Parents' Influence.

Daddy's car accident that ended his life on earth was and is the greatest tragedy of my life. I was sixteen and a half. Daddy was fifty-three years of age.

Daddy always treated me like a big girl. He taught me

to read when my teacher and brothers could not. And one time Daddy said to me, "Don't let being a girl keep you from doing what you want to do." I haven't.

Daddy and I talked about the Bible and how to get to heaven. After Daddy had passed on, I had a dream that he came down to visit me. He said, "I just thought I'd come down and see you for a while." I believe God sent me the dream to ease my pain of missing Daddy.

Mom was the greatest influence on my early life. During the depression when times were so hard, Mom spent her time cooking for our large family and, most of the time, singing hymns and folk songs in her beautiful soprano voice. She never seemed depressed.

Mom taught me to appreciate life. Before I started school, she taught me a poem that let me know I was where God wanted me to be.

Herb and Anna Lacey - 1926 wedding

196

Our Family Memories.

Not long after Bill and I were married, we soon started our family. By the time we were married five years, we had our two boys and two girls, just as I had dreamed.

Bill and I started our life together, living in a camper. With the addition of our kids to our family, over time, we moved to two rental homes. Then we purchased a home in Kirksville, Missouri. We lived in Kirksville for ten years.

Because of Bill's work, we moved to Wichita in 1960 where Mom and many of my family lived. We bought a large Victorian home close to schools and Bill's work. And our families had many long Saturday night square dances. It was a fun time for all.

Bill worked for a dairy, and we enjoyed all the ice cream we wanted. I began my sewing business and made a little extra cash for some extras for our family. Then I started working for an antique shop where I acquired many beautiful pieces of antique furniture for our Victorian home.

We were attending a church close by and had many parties for kids and teens at our house. There were many neighborhood kids and youth who also attended our church and enjoyed our parties. Our house was their favorite place to "party."

For our 25th Wedding Anniversary, Bill and I celebrated at home with our kids and grandkids, with a huge dinner for family and a reception in the afternoon with friends and neighbors.

Bill and Bonnie - 25th anniversary

Our kids were growing up fast. Over the years, our family took many great vacations together. We visited my brother's horse ranch in Colorado for a week before school started and always had an exciting time. Sometimes on school breaks, our family visited Bill's parents and uncle in the country in Missouri. We have wonderful memories of our family vacations.

My Next Dreams.

As our kids were finishing school, I began my dream of becoming a nurse. Bill didn't understand my determination to do it. Still, he threw his support behind me and would say, "Go for it!" During that time, I read a paper and wrote a poem: LIVING.

After becoming a nurse, guess what? I worked on fulfilling another childhood dream.

Bonnie and Cessna 150

I started learning to fly the airplane Bill and I bought, a Cessna 150, for both of us to learn to fly. I took lessons and eventually earned my pilot's license. By then we had grandkids who went on morning flights with me.

Bill and I took many vacations after our kids grew up and left home. We visited historic sites, including several former presidents' homes. He had loved to drive over-the-road for his job, and was always glad to be "on the road again." One favorite place was Mountain View, Arkansas.

I decided, with Bill's approval, to start back to college for my master's degree in nursing, while working there as a Graduate Teacher's Assistant. I earned my Nurse Practitioner's License (NP), later known as Advanced Practice Registered Nurse (APRN). And, because Bill chose not to get his pilot's license, we sold our Cessna 150. I had fulfilled my dream of becoming a pilot.

Some Drastic Changes.

Everything changed when Bill suffered a heart attack and had to have triple-bypass surgery. He had to retire but received great benefits through the Teamster Union. He recovered well and insisted that I finish my master's degree and graduate.

Now that Bill was retired, he wanted to move to the country. We found a house at Lake Waltanna and moved just as I finished my master's degree. Bill planned a surprise graduation party with our kids, my extended family, and friends.

I worked in many areas of nursing practice, eventually accepting a position as a school nurse. Retiring from full-time nursing when I was sixty-eight years of age. I continued to work in part-time positions until I was seventy-nine.

A Special Time.

Our 50th Wedding Anniversary was a huge event. First Bill and I celebrated with our kids and grandkids at our home. Then we rented a ballroom where we celebrated with extended family and friends for two days.

Bill and I had over twenty houseguests for several days and the attendance at the ballroom was over four hundred. We renewed our vows and celebrated by singing, dancing, and feasting on food provided by the ballroom.

Bill and Bonnie 1999 renewing vows

Mission Trip to Turkey.

When I mentioned to Bill about wanting to take a three-week mission trip with a local group to Ephesus, Turkey, he smiled and said, "Go for it!" Our group would hold Bible school for the children of our denomination's workers there, while they held their bi-annual meeting.

The trip was in August, after our 50th Wedding Anniversary. Besides doing Bible school, we had time to tour historic Ephesus and take a cruise to the Isle of Patmos. The mission trip was a grand experience and I'm pleased I did it.

Another Big Change.

Now drawing Social Security, I retired from nursing full time. I kept my nursing license current until my ninetieth birthday, just because I wanted to.

Another change was coming. Our swimming pool

caved in on one side, and we had to fill it in. One less task for Bill; keeping the pool clean. And we noticed we had fewer guests.

Bill was driving twenty miles to town to his doctor more frequently. One day, he suggested we move back to Wichita. Our new home there on West 19th Street was a nearly new one-story with a full basement, a first for us.

Our kids and grandkids enjoyed our new home. Also, as our extended families and friends heard about our home, we had a constant stream of visitors, which we loved. It was good to be back in Wichita.

We filled our few years there with wonderful memories of our family. Bill's health, however, was declining. Only he and I knew. He didn't want others to know, but our kids suspected. We both looked forward to our trips to Mountain View each spring and fall, realizing each trip may be the last time we could go. It was the only time we could be alone, together, without phone calls or drop-in guests.

Even more precious were our family get-togethers with our kids and grandkids for the holidays and birthdays. The family get-togethers just got bigger and better each year.

Sadly, the time came for Bill to leave us, as God called him home to heaven. During our time of grief and mourning, I had to make decisions without Bill. Within a few months, I sold our house and moved my home to an apartment in a senior retirement complex.

Continuing with My Life.

Shortly after moving, I got a phone call from a niece,

my sister's daughter, in North Carolina. She and her fiancé were getting married in a hot-air balloon and invited me to attend the ceremony in the air with them. It had been a fun tip. I felt honored that they invited me to take the balloon ride with them. Or maybe no one else wanted to go.

Mission Trip to China.

I heard at my church about a mission trip a group of men and women were taking to China in December. They invited me to go along. We couldn't go to China as missionaries, but we were to stay on a college campus and speak English with students to improve their English-speaking skills.

So, our group of women and men flew to New York City, then flew up over Canada and down to China to the Beijing Airport. From there, we took a chartered bus to the college campus, where we stayed in dorms with our workers and students.

After two weeks with the students, our group took a on a sight-seeing tour of China. We visited the magnificent Terra Cotta Soldiers' Museum and the historic Tiananmen Square.

Most of all, I wanted to walk on the Great Wall of China. Finally, our bus took us there. Our group walked together, up the uneven, hand-hewn steps for about a mile. As we looked out over the beautiful mountains and forests below us, it looked to me like we were on top of the world. Who else can say they walked on the Great Wall of China?

This trip and experiences were some of the greatest

of my life. We got home a few days before Christmas. My family showed up as always for our first Christmas without Bill. We celebrated his life.

It's Not Over Yet!

My apartment was an upper level three-bedroom with a balcony. After the holidays, I moved to a ground level, two-bedroom apartment where we could walk out my sliding door onto the lawn by the lake. Our grandkids spent many happy hours playing there in the summer. Some grumpy neighbors, though, complained about the joyful noises of the kids.

I found an apartment complex where there were families and moved the following May to a one-bedroom apartment. After settling in, I began digging flower beds. I planted summer blooming flowers and perennials that would bloom the following year. The flowers are still blooming after twelve years.

With our large family and my lack of space for our family Christmas, I contracted with a local buffet restaurant to meet there for our buffet dinner. My friend, Santa, showed up as usual with gifts. And now our kids and grandkids invite me to their family celebrations. It is a busy, happy time.

I have spent several years writing my memoirs, up to the present time. Only God knows how many years I have left before departing this life. I have always wanted to follow Jesus and be the best wife, mother, and grandmother. I believe I can say I have fought the good fight. I have finished the course. I have kept the faith (2 Timothy 4: 7).

But it's not over yet!

Bonnie and Bill Through the Years

1947

1999

2005

Bonnie Lacey Krenning

1932

1947

1976

WICHITA STATE UNIVERSITY
Commencement
May 21, 1988

1988

Bonnie Lacey Krenning

2009

Made in the USA
Middletown, DE
14 September 2023

38252376R00116